The Sensitive Body Cookbook

Delicious and Nutritious Gluten Free, Lactose Free, Soy Free, and Citrus Free Recipes

By Virginia Van Royen

TABLE OF CONTENTS

Introduction..p 4-6

Ch. 1
Ingredients Preparation.....................................p 7-9

Ch. 2
Stocks, Sauces, and Salad Dressings...................p 10-18

Ch. 3
Soups, Stews, and Salads.................................p 19-35

Ch. 4
Egg Recipes..p 36-45

Ch. 5
Fruits and Vegetables Snacks and Meals...............p 46-54

Ch. 6
Rice & Potatoes Recipes..................................p 55-66

Ch. 7
Poultry..p 67-88

Ch. 8
Beef...p 89-98

Ch. 9
Desserts and Snacks.......................................p 99-112

Appendix A
List of foods not in the cookbook........................p 113

Appendix B
List of Foods in the cookbook............................p 114-115

Appendix C
Five week dinner list..p 116-117

Index p118-128

Introduction

This cookbook is a result of years of suffering with chronic migraines, and the unpleasant side effects of a variety of medications prescribed in unsuccessful efforts at remediation, which led me to research and find solutions through changes in my diet. I am not a chef, doctor, or professional nutritionist. This book is simply based on my personal experiences. There are many excellent cookbooks written for migraine reduction. The best book I have read to help me adjust my diet to reduce migraines was recommended by my neurologist: "Heal Your Headache. The 1-2-3 Program" by David Buchholz, MD. Also, there are lots of cookbooks out there with helpful recipes and food ideas that were also a helpful start: "The Primal Blueprint Diet" by Mark Sission with Jennifer Meier; "The Headache Prevention Cookbook" by David R. Marks MD and Laura Marks, M.D.; the "Migraine Gourmet" by Jerry Rainville; and "The Fibromyalgia Cookbook" by Shelly Ann Smith.

The big challenge is that we all have different food sensitivities. I have solved this problem by using the elimination diet, which basically is a procedure used to identify foods that may be causing an adverse effect in a person, in which all suspected foods are excluded from the diet and then reintroduced one at a time. I ended up with quite a limited diet, and very little processed food. The hardest part is attending parties where there is nothing I can eat without getting a bad bowel upset or a migraine. This is why I decided to come up with these yummy recipes to share with others who have food sensitivities, and who want to bring gluten free, nut free, soy free, lactose free snacks to parties. At these parties, people have been surprised at how tasty these treats can be, and have requested a copy of the recipe from me.

In Appendix A is the list of foods I *cannot* eat. If you would like to see the foods that will be in this cookbook, check out Appendix B, it is the list of foods I have come up with that I *can* eat. Appendix C shows a one month dinner list. Chapter Two shows some food prep tips which can help reduce the amount of time it takes to make meals, especially breakfast.

Every recipe I have created comes from eliminating foods I cannot eat, or reducing the number of times per week I can have some foods. You too can adapt recipes to your personal needs by changing/adjusting foods you do not tolerate. For example, butter is on the edge of lactose intolerance. Some of us can handle it, some of us cannot, and sometimes tolerance levels change. Replacements for butter in many recipes can be margarine or coconut oil. I have replaced nuts with seeds. If nuts are not a dietary problem for you, choose your favorite nuts to replace the sunflower seeds and pumpkin seeds. If your body can't handle kale, replace it with spinach. No cauliflower? Try broccoli. The key is to experiment with cooking by altering various parts/ingredients so your body can tolerate it.

Some examples of my food replacements:
-Nuts are replaced by a variety of seeds
-Wheat is replaced by Brown Rice Flour or Gluten Free Flour with ingredients I can handle such as potato starch and rice flour
-Onions are replaced with shallots or scallions
-Very few spices are used, but a significant number of herbs are used
-Milk is replaced with rice milk, and occasionally coconut milk, and almond milk can work for those who can eat nuts
-Soy sauce is replaced with a migraine free non-soy sauce substitute (see page 18)
-Bread is replaced with gluten free bread. After a search through many brands I have found the one that does not contain ingredients I can't handle. You find the one that works for you
-Peanut butter is replaced with sunflower butter
-Basic salt is replaced with sea salt
-Refined sugar is replaced with turbinado raw cane sugar, honey, or molasses
-Wine in recipes is replaced with grape juice or apple juice
-Fancy vinegars with migraine ingredients are replaced with basic White Vinegar or Apple Cider Vinegar (which is supposed to be helpful for migraines)

-Lemon juice and orange juice are replaced with apple juice, cranberry juice, or grape juice, because citrus products can be migraine triggers

-In baking with eggs, if eggs are intolerable, you can replace each egg with 1 tablespoon of whole ground flax seeds that have soaked for 30 minutes or more in 3 tablespoons of water

A note on cooking times for recipes: ovens and burners vary in their time to heat up, and amount of real heat at each level. Gas stoves and burners cook with different timing than electric stoves and burners. It is important to know your stove and burners, because it can affect cooking times. Keep an eye on your foods as they cook. My cooking times are based on an electric stove and burners.

A note on iron skillets: iron skillets are listed in my recipes, but you can use the skillet of your choice. Iron skillets take a little longer to heat up, but hold the heat as ingredients are added. They must be dried with a towel or paper towel after being washed. There is a lot of information about how to take care of iron skillets on-line, and any iron skillet you may purchase will usually come with instructions. I have a basic set of 3 iron skillets, small, medium (deep, great for stews), and large.

Margarine is a choice for lactose free recipes. If you can tolerate lactose, you can replace the margarine with butter. When using margarine instead of butter for vegan choices, check labels. When looking for a vegan margarine, beware of whey, lactose, casein and caseinate, which are dairy derivatives frequently used in margarines. Many margarines contain soy, but if you are soy tolerant, no problem. I like Earth Balance soy free butter sticks for baked snacks.

A positive side effect of these recipes over the years has been a large reduction in my cholesterol level, which went from way too high to just right. Finally, and really to repeat myself, enjoy the recipes I have here, and feel free to experiment with them. I've tried to leave lots of margin spaces for your notes!

Chapter 1

Ingredients Preparation

One of the most helpful things I find in my cooking is pre-made ingredients. Here are the "recipes" for preparing some ingredients ahead of time:

Bread Crumbs
Toast 2-4 slices of gluten free bread until lightly brown. Cool slightly. Break into smaller pieces as you place them in a blender. Blend off and on until breadcrumbs are of the desired crumb size. Place in container or zip lock bag and store in refrigerator up to 7 days, or freezer up to three months.

Cilantro or Parsley
Rinse parsley or cilantro in colander. Place ¼ of them on a chopping board. Slice off stems. To a use a knife to chop parsley, hold the back edge of the tip down with your non-dominant hand. The dominant hand will obviously be holding the handle of the knife! Then, holding the tip in place, move your dominant hand up and down, working around the pile of parsley or cilantro until it is cut to your liking. Place in a glass container to refrigerate up to 7 days, or freeze for 2 months.

Chopped Celery
Open up and wash each celery stalk. Slice each stalk into four lengthwise pieces. Line up 8-16 of these, and slice into mini cubes. Place in container or zip lock bag and store in refrigerator up to 7 days, or freezer up to two months.

Fruits Sliced and Frozen
When fruits such as grapes, strawberries, apricots, or any other fruit you enjoy is looking like it needs to be eaten in the next 24 hours, but you have an overabundance, they may be prepared to freeze. I use frozen fruits for home veggie-fruit shakes, so the freezer is a great place to save them. Wash the fruit, and slice into a good size (i.e. strawberries in half, grapes I don't slice). Spread fruit slices on a cookie sheet, and place in the freezer for one hour. After one hour, put the frozen fruit into a zip lock bag or storage container and store it in the freezer up to 6 weeks.

Gluten Free Oatmeal Flour
If you'd like to make your own, buy a large bag of gluten free oatmeal. Place 1 cup of this in a blender, and blend off and on until gluten free oatmeal is grated into a flour level. Store in a zip lock bag or glass container.

Red, Orange, or Yellow Bell Peppers
Slice off top, pull out seeds, and wash with water. Slice lengthwise, then into cubes. Freeze in zip lock bag for up to 2 months.

Shredded Carrots
Wash 4 carrots and peel with peeler. Cut off ends. Over a large bowl, shred with cheese shredder. When all are shredded, spread out on a cookie sheet and freeze for 1 hour. After freezing, place in container or zip lock bag and store in freezer for up to two months.

Shredded Zucchini
Wash 2-4 zucchini. Cut off ends. Over a large bowl, shred with cheese shredder, then spread the shreds out on a cookie sheet and freeze for 1 hour. After freezing, place in container or zip lock bag and store in freezer for up to two months.

Sliced Leeks
Slice 2 leeks in half lengthwise. Thoroughly rinse in a colander. Place on cutting board and slice each half in half lengthwise, so both leeks are "quartered." Lineup four quarters at a time, and slice into $1/8$" slices. Place in container or zip lock bag and refrigerate for up to 7 days, or freeze up to 2 months.

Sliced Scallions (long green onions)
I like to use the whole scallion. Rinse 8-12 scallions. Cut off a little of each end (roots & tips). Line up 4-8 scallions and slice as thinly or thickly as you like. I do about $1/8$ of an inch. Place in container or zip lock bag and refrigerate for up to 7 days, or freeze up to 3 months.

Spaghetti Squash
I prep and freeze this for omelets. Spaghetti squash is an excellent replacement for pasta, so I often have leftovers to freeze. To cook spaghetti squash, cut in half, remove seeds, and microwave each half separately for 8 minutes each. Let cool for 5 minutes, then use a fork to scrape out the spaghetti squash strands into a bowl or large plate. When all are pulled out, spread out on a cookie sheet and freeze for 1 hour. After freezing, pull together and place in container or zip lock bag and store in freezer for up to two months.

Chapter 2

Stocks, Sauces, and Salad Dressings

When making stocks, I freeze them in one-cup amounts in small glass containers.

Beef Stock

4 cups water
1 cup beef bones and/or beef fat cut from steaks
1 celery stalk, cut into big slices
4 shallots, chopped into big slices
½ cup parsley
2 bay leaves
1 tsp. sea salt
¼ tsp. paprika

1. Place all ingredients in a cooking pot.
2. Bring to boil, cover and reduce to simmer for 1 hour.
3. Remove from heat and let cool for 10-20 minutes.
4. Drain liquid into a bowl through a colander. Save stock in a glass container.
5. May be refrigerated for up to 7 days, frozen up to 3 months.

Chicken Stock

I make this recipe after cooking a whole chicken, using the bones and any internal parts left over.

4 cups water
1 leftover baked chicken bones
3 shallots, chopped in big slices
1 celery stalk, chopped in big slices
1 carrot, chopped in big slices
½ cup parsley
1 tsp. sea salt
1/4 tsp. pepper

1. Place all ingredients in a cooking pot.
2. Bring to a boil, cover and reduce to simmer for 1 hour.
3. Remove from heat and let cool for 10-20 minutes.
4. Drain liquid into a bowl through a colander. Save stock in a glass container.
5. May be refrigerated for up to 7 days, frozen up to 3 months.

Veggie Stock   **VEGAN**

4 cups water
2 large carrots, chopped in big slices
2 celery stalks, chopped in big slices
1 large tomato, chopped in big slices
2 shallots, chopped in big slices
½ a leek, chopped in big slices
4 garlic cloves, chopped in big slices
½ cup parsley
2 bay leaves
1 tsp. thyme
1 tsp. sea salt

1. Place all ingredients in a cooking pot.
2. Bring to a boil, cover and reduce heat to simmer for 1 hour.
3. Remove from heat and let cool for 10-20 minutes.
4. Drain liquid into a bowl through a colander. Save stock in a glass container.
5. May be refrigerated for up to 7 days, frozen up to 3 months.

Homemade Gravy

3 Tbsp. margarine
3 Tbsp. gluten free flour
1 cup beef stock
¼ tsp. sea salt
¼ tsp. pepper

1. Melt margarine in a small pot on low heat.
2. Mix in gluten free flour.
3. Slowly blend in beef stock, salt, and pepper.
4. Raise temperature to boil, stirring frequently. As the gravy thickens, reduce heat to simmer and cook for five minutes with stirring.
5. Serve.

(Note: an alternative to gluten free flour is 3 Tbsp. corn starch and 3 Tbsp. water.)

Apple Cider Dressing 　　　　　　**8 servings**　　　　**VEGAN**

⅓ cup olive oil
⅓ cup apple cider vinegar
¼ cup turbinado sugar
½ tsp. sea salt
2 sliced scallions

1. Place all ingredients in cooking pot and bring to a boil.
2. Reduce heat to medium low and cook and stir for five minutes.
3. Remove from heat and refrigerate for one hour, then place in airtight container.
4. Can be stored in refrigerator for up to 14 days.

Apple Juice Dressing   **4 servings**   **VEGAN**

2 Tbsp. apple juice
1 Tbsp. olive oil
1 Tbsp. white vinegar
1 tsp. dried basil
1 clove garlic, minced
Freshly ground black pepper

1. Place all ingredients in a small glass container.
2. Mix with a spoon or fork.
3. Refrigerate three hours before serving.

Honey Mustard Dressing   **4 servings**   **VEGAN**

2 Tbsp. white vinegar
2 Tbsp. olive oil
2 tsp. Dijon mustard
1 tsp. honey

1. Place all ingredients in a small glass container.
2. Mix with a spoon or fork.
3. Refrigerate three hours before serving.

Sesame Salad Dressing 4 servings

2 Tbsp. olive oil
1 Tbsp. apple cider vinegar
2 Tbsp. white vinegar
1 tsp. sesame oil
1 tsp. sesame seeds
1 Tbsp. soy sauce substitute (page 18)
1 clove crushed garlic
½ tsp. sea salt

1. Place all ingredients in a small glass container.
2. Mix with a spoon or fork.
3. Store in refrigerator up to 4 weeks.
4. Shake before using in a salad.

Soy Sauce Substitute

This "soy sauce" works in cooking. It is not intended to replace soy sauce as a condiment.

1 ½ cups beef stock (page 10)
1 Tbsp. white vinegar
1 dash ground black pepper
1 Tbsp. dark molasses
¼ cup apple cider vinegar
1 Tbsp. sesame oil
1 tsp. sea salt

1. Place all ingredients in a cooking pot and bring to a boil.
2. Reduce heat to low and simmer for 20 minutes.
3. Remove from heat, pour into an airtight jar, and seal.
4. Store in refrigerator.
5. Shake well before using.

CHAPTER 3

Soups, Stews, and Salads

Beef Barley Stew   **6 servings**

¼ cup gluten free flour
¼ tsp. pepper
½ tsp. sea salt
1 lb. sliced beef
4 Tbsp. margarine or olive oil
2 shallots, chopped
2 garlic cloves, crushed
1 cup sliced green beans
1 cup sliced carrots
4-6 cups beef stock
1 bay leaf
1 tsp. oregano
1 tsp. sea salt
¾ cup barley

1. Mix gluten free flour, ½ tsp. salt and ¼ tsp. pepper in a large flat bowl or other container.
2. Cover beef with flour mix by rolling around in bowl or container.
3. Place butter or olive oil in pot on medium heat.
4. Sauté flour covered beef to brown, about 5 minutes.
5. Add shallots and cook for 2 minutes
6. Add garlic cloves and cook and stir for another 2 minutes.
7. Add veggies, beef broth, herbs, 1 tsp. salt, and barley.
8. Mix and bring to a boil.
9. Reduce heat to low, cover and simmer for 1 hour.
10. Remove lid, remove bay leaf, stir, and serve.

Beef Stew, Old Fashioned   **6 servings**

12 oz. beef steak, trimmed and cut into 1" cubes
4 Tbsp. gluten free flour
½ tsp. sea salt
¼ tsp. pepper
2 Tbsp. olive oil
4 shallots, chopped
8 mushrooms, sliced
3 cloves garlic, crushed
¼ tsp. thyme
½ cup apple juice
1 Tbsp. cooking sherry or soy sauce substitute (page 18)
2 cups beef stock (page 10)
¼ cup tomato paste
2 potatoes cut into small cubes
1 cup carrots, sliced
½ cup water
2 Tbsp. dried parsley or ¼ cup fresh chopped parsley

1. Mix gluten free flour, ½ tsp. salt and ¼ tsp. pepper in a large flat bowl or other container.
2. Cover beef with flour mix by rolling around in bowl or container.
3. Place 1 Tbsp. olive oil in a Dutch oven on medium heat.
4. Sauté shallots for 2 minutes. Add garlic and sauté for 1 minute
5. Add flour covered beef and cook to brown about 10 minutes.
6. Add 1 Tbsp. olive oil and the mushrooms, and sauté, stirring every minute or so, for 3 minutes.
7. Add thyme, apple juice, cooking sherry, beef broth, and tomato paste, scrape up any brown bits from bottom of pan, and add in any left-over gluten free flour from beef-flour mix.
8. Add potatoes, carrots, water, and parsley.

9. Bring to a boil, reduce heat, and cover to simmer for one hour and 15 minutes.
10. Remove lid, stir, and serve.

Chicken Soup   **4 servings**

1 Tbsp. olive oil
1 diced shallot
2 cloves crushed garlic
1 celery stalk, diced
2 chicken breasts, cubed
1 cup sliced carrots
½ cup sliced green beans
½ cup sliced mushrooms (optional ingredient)
½ tsp. sea salt
¼ tsp. thyme
¼ tsp. oregano
4 cups chicken stock (page 11)
1 cup cooked brown Basmati rice or uncooked rice pasta

1. In large cooking pot, on medium heat, add oil and diced shallot, cook for 1 minute.
2. Add garlic and celery, and cook for 5 minutes with stirring every minute.
3. Add chicken breast cubes and sauté until fully cooked, stirring every minute or so.
4. Add carrots, green beans (optional mushrooms) salt, thyme and oregano and cook, stirring every minute for 5 minutes.
5. Add chicken stock and 1 cup cooked brown rice or uncooked rice pasta.
6. Bring to a boil, reduce heat, and cover.
7. Simmer for 20 minutes.
8. Remove lid, stir, and serve.

Chili Con Carne　　　　　　　　　　　　　　　**4 servings**

2 scallions, finely chopped
2 Tbsp. olive oil
1 lb. ground beef
14 oz. can slice tomatoes
4 Tbsp. tomato paste
1 tsp. sea salt
1 tsp. marjoram
1 tsp. caraway seed
1 bay leaf
½ cup water
14 oz. can of cooked organic black beans, rinsed

1. Sauté scallions in oil in cooking pot, or deep iron skillet, for five minutes.
2. Add beef and fully cook.
3. Add tomatoes, tomato paste, sea salt, marjoram, caraway seed, bay leaf, and water.
4. Bring to a boil.
5. Reduce heat to low and cover.
6. Simmer covered for 20 minutes.
7. Add black beans and simmer for 10 more minutes.
8. Serve

Hearty Sausage & Bean Soup   **4 servings**

1 lb. turkey sausage (page 87)
1 shallot, chopped
1 Tbsp. olive oil
2 cups cooked black beans (or one 14oz can, rinsed)
3 cups water or veggie stock
1 can chopped tomatoes
½ cup red or yellow bell peppers, chopped
1 large bay leaf
½ tsp. sea salt
½ tsp. thyme
¼ tsp. garlic powder (or 1 garlic clove crushed)
¼ tsp. pepper

1. In large cooking pot, cook turkey sausage and shallots in olive oil over medium heat.
2. Once cooked, add in all other ingredients, stir, and bring to a boil.
3. Cover, reduce heat, and simmer for 1 hour.
4. Remove lid and stir, ready to serve.

Turkey Sausage Soup 2 servings

½ lb. cooked turkey sausage (page 87)
1 cup chicken stock
1 cup spaghetti squash, precooked (page 9)
3/4 cup sliced roasted tomatoes (or ½ can roasted tomatoes)
¼ cup parsley, finely chopped
¼ tsp. basil
1 clove garlic, crushed

1. Place cooking pot over medium heat.
2. Pour in all ingredients, stir every minute or so as you bring to a boil.
3. Reduce heat and bring to simmer. Cook for 5 more minutes.
4. Serve in soup bowls.

Black Bean Salad 2 servings **VEGAN**

¼ cup cooked organic black beans
3 Tbsp. diced tomatoes or red bell peppers
3 kalamata olives, sliced (or olives of your choice)
3 green olives, sliced
2 cups organic salad greens
3 sliced basil leaves
Honey Mustard Dressing (page 16)

1. In a medium sized bowl, combine all ingredients, mix thoroughly, and serve.

Broccoli Slaw Salad 4 servings **VEGAN**

1 cup shredded broccoli stalk
1 cup shredded carrots
¼ cup dried cranberries
¼ cup roasted/salted sunflower seeds
1 cup apples, diced
Honey Mustard Salad dressing (page 16)

1. In a medium sized mixing bowl, combine all ingredients and mix thoroughly.

Chicken Salad   **6 servings**

1 Tbsp. olive oil
½ tsp. sea salt
2 chicken breasts, cubed
6 cups organic salad greens
1 cup shredded carrots
1 cup shredded broccoli stalk or apple
1 cup shredded steamed & peeled beets
½ cup dried cranberries
½ cup sunflower seeds
6 Tbsp. apple cider dressing (page 14)

1. Place olive oil in skillet over medium heat.
2. Add salt and cubed chicken breasts and sauté for 10 minutes, stirring occasionally.
3. When fully cooked, remove from skillet and place in refrigerator for 20 minutes to cool.
4. In large salad bowl, blend baby spring mix lettuce, shredded carrots, shredded broccoli stock or apple, shredded beets, dried cranberries, and sunflower seeds.
5. When chicken is cooled, add to salad mix.
6. Add 6 tablespoons of apple cider dressing and blend.
7. Serve.

Chinese Chicken Salad   4 servings

1 Tbsp. olive oil
½ tsp. sea salt
2 chicken breasts, cubed
4 cups organic salad greens, sliced
¼ cup dry rice noodles or crushed rice crackers
2 Tbsp. sunflower seeds (or sliced almonds if you can tolerate nuts)
2 scallions, sliced

Dressing

1 Tbsp. sesame seeds, toasted
2 Tbsp. sunflower seed oil or olive oil
1 Tbsp. white vinegar
1 tsp. sesame oil
1 Tbsp. turbinado sugar or honey
1 garlic clove, crushed
¼ tsp. sea salt
2 dashes of pepper
1 Tbsp. apple juice

1. Place olive oil in skillet over medium heat.
2. Add salt and cubed chicken breasts and sauté for 10 minutes, stirring occasionally.
3. When fully cooked, remove from skillet and place in refrigerator for 20 minutes to cool.
4. Mix all ingredients in a large bowl.
5. Mix all dressing ingredients with a whisk, until well mixed.
6. Add dressing to salad, blend, and serve.

Cranberry Tuna Salad **2 servings**

12 oz. canned tuna, drained
1 celery stalk, finely chopped
1 shallot, finely chopped
¼ cup mayonnaise
¼ cup dried cranberries

1. Mix all ingredients together in a bowl until well blended.
2. Serve.

Mediterranean Salad 4 servings **VEGAN**

4 cups chopped romaine lettuce
1 medium tomato, sliced
1 small cucumber, sliced
4 scallions, chopped
4 radishes, cubed
¼ cup parsley, finely chopped

Dressing

2 Tbsp. olive oil
1 Tbsp. apple cider vinegar
1 Tbsp. apple juice
¼ tsp. sea salt
¼ tsp. pepper

1. Combine all veggie ingredients in a large bowl and toss well
2. Mix olive oil, cider vinegar, apple juice, salt and pepper in a small bowl or cup.
3. Serve salad with dressing on the side, or add dressing to salad and mix well.

Mixed Bean Salad   **4 servings**   **VEGAN**

1 cup green beans
1 cup cooked black beans
2 sliced beets
½ red, yellow, or orange bell pepper, sliced

1. Mix all ingredients in a medium sized bowl.
2. Add Apple Cider dressing (page 14), blend, and serve.
3. Can be refrigerated for up to two days.

Stacker Salad   **2 servings**   **VEGAN**

1 large tomato, sliced into 6 slices
1 Tbsp. chopped basil
4 slices cucumber
1 shallot sliced into 8 rings
1 Tbsp. olive oil
2 Tbsp. apple juice
¼ tsp. sea salt
2 dashes pepper

1. Combine olive oil, apple juice, salt, and pepper in a small bowl or cup and set aside this dressing.
2. To make stacker, begin with tomato slice, top with basil, cucumber slice, onion ring, and one more tomato slice. Make four stacks.
3. Drizzle dressing over four stacks and serve.

Turkey Salad **4 servings**

1 Tbsp. olive oil
½ tsp. sea salt
2 cups turkey, cubed
2 stalks celery, diced
2 scallions, sliced
½ red bell pepper, diced
3 Tbsp. mayonnaise
1 Tbsp. apple cider vinegar
1 tsp. turbinado sugar
¼ tsp. sea salt
2 cups lettuce of your choice

1. Place olive oil in skillet over medium heat.
2. Add salt and cubed turkey and sauté for 10 minutes, stirring occasionally.
3. When fully cooked, remove from skillet and place in refrigerator for 20 minutes to cool.
4. Blend cooled turkey, celery, scallions, and bell pepper.
5. In separate bowl, mix mayonnaise, vinegar, sugar and salt until well blended.
6. Pour dressing over turkey mix and blend.
7. When well mixed place over lettuce.

Waldorf Chicken Salad **4 servings**

1 Tbsp. olive oil
½ tsp. sea salt
2 chicken breasts, cubed
2 celery stalks, thinly sliced
1 small apple, diced
⅓ cup halved seedless grapes
¼ cup sunflower seeds (or walnuts if you are ok with nuts)
¼ cup mayonnaise
3 cups organic salad greens

1. Place olive oil in skillet over medium heat.
2. Add salt and cubed chicken and sauté for 10 minutes, stirring occasionally.
3. When fully cooked, remove from skillet and place in refrigerator for 20 minutes to cool.
4. In large bowl combine first cooled cooked chicken, sliced celery, diced apple, halved grapes, sunflower seed and mayonnaise.
5. Mix well and serve over organic salad greens.

CHAPTER 4

Egg Recipes

These can be made for breakfast or for dinner.

Broccoli Quiche   **2 servings**

1 tsp. olive oil
4 broccoli florets, sliced into small pieces (just about 1 cup)
3 eggs
1/4 cup rice milk
1 Tbsp. margarine, melted
⅛ tsp. nutmeg
1 sprinkle of pepper
¼ tsp. sea salt

1. Place olive oil in small iron skillet on medium heat.
2. Preheat oven to broil.
3. Cook broccoli in skillet for 4 minutes.
4. Whisk together eggs, rice milk, melted margarine, nutmeg, salt, and pepper.
5. Pour onto broccoli in iron skillet.
6. Cover with lid and cook for 5 minutes.
7. Place on bottom rack of oven and broil for 5 minutes.
8. Remove from oven, slice in half, and serve.

Carrot Scrambled Eggs   **2 servings**

2 tsp. olive oil
1 Tbsp. chopped celery stalk
¼ cup shredded carrot
1 Tbsp. scallion, chopped
3 eggs
¼ tsp. sea salt
2 dashes pepper

1. Place olive oil in iron skillet on medium heat for one minute.
2. Add celery, carrot, and scallion. Sauté for 5 minutes.
3. Whisk together eggs, salt, and pepper and pour into iron skillet with vegetables.
4. Cook while pushing with a spatula every 40-60 seconds, until eggs are done.
5. Optional: serve over hash browns or gluten free toast.

Kale or Bok Choy Scrambled Eggs   2 servings

1 tsp. olive oil
1 small shallot, chopped
¼ red bell pepper, cubed
1 handful fresh kale or Bok Choy
3 eggs
¼ tsp. sea salt
⅛ tsp. oregano
1 dash of pepper

1. Place olive oil in iron skillet on medium heat for one minute.
2. Sauté shallots and peppers for five minutes.
3. Add Kale and cook for a few more minutes until the leaves shrink way down.
4. Whisk eggs, salt, and pepper.
5. Pour into skillet on sautéed ingredients and cook while pushing with a spatula every minute or so until eggs are done.
6. Delicious served on cooked hash browns or toasted gluten free bread.

Leeks Scrambled Eggs   **2 servings**

1 tsp. olive oil
2 Tbsp. split & sliced leeks
3 eggs
2 hash browns

1. Cook hash browns in oven.
2. Place olive oil in iron skillet on medium heat for one minute.
3. Sauté leeks until light brown, about five minutes.
4. Remove from skillet and place on plate.
5. Whisk eggs and cook in skillet.
6. Place hash browns on serving plates, place cooked scrambled eggs on hash browns, and place cooked leeks on top.
7. Sprinkle with salt.

Pizza Frittata 2 servings

1 Tbsp. olive oil
3 options, choose your favorite:
    1 turkey sausage (page 87) or
    2 homemade beef bacon (page 89) or
    1/2 cup sliced ground meat
3 mushrooms, sliced
1 medium tomato, sliced into cubes
3 beaten eggs
¼ cup fresh basil
1/4 tsp. oregano

1. Preheat broiler.
2. Place olive oil in iron skillet on medium heat for one minute.
3. Add mushrooms and meat and sauté until mushrooms are soft and moisture has evaporated.
4. Add tomatoes and sauté 1 minute.
5. Whisk eggs and pour in skillet and sprinkle with oregano and basil.
6. Stir quickly, then cook undisturbed until eggs begin to set.
7. Place frittata under broiler until top is golden and eggs are firm (2-4 minutes).
8. Sprinkle with salt and pepper to taste. If you're not lactose intolerant, sprinkle with cheese of your choice.

Quiche   **4 servings**

1 tsp. olive oil
5-10 crushed rice crackers
3 mushrooms, chopped
2 scallions, chopped
1 cup of vegetables, chopped (possibilities: spinach, Bok Choy, broccoli, cauliflower, green beans, kale, roasted bell pepper, shredded carrots, and zucchini)
5-6 eggs (whites separated)
1 tsp. Italian herbs
10 grinds pepper
½ tsp. sea salt

1. Preheat oven at 375 degrees F.
2. Spread 1 Tbsp. olive oil in medium iron skillet.
3. Spread crushed rice crackers in the bottom of oiled pie pan or medium iron skillet.
4. Mix mushrooms, scallions, and veggies in a small bowl, then spread evenly over rice crackers.
5. Whisk egg yolks with Italian herbs, pepper, and salt.
6. Separately whip egg whites until slightly fluffy, and fold into egg yolk mixture.
7. Pour eggs over veggies in pie plate (or iron skillet). Place in oven and bake for 20 minutes.

Spaghetti Squash Omelet   2 servings

1 tsp. olive oil
1/4 cup cooked spaghetti squash (p 9)
3 eggs
1 Tbsp. olive oil
1 sliced scallion
Choose sea salt and pepper to taste

1. Whisk eggs.
2. Add spaghetti squash, salt, pepper, and scallion.
3. Place olive oil in iron skillet on medium heat for one minute.
4. Add egg mix to pan, and let cook 1 min.
5. Put lid on pan and cook for 1-2 minutes more.
6. Use a spatula to gently turn over omelet. Cook for 2-3 minutes longer.
7. Gently remove from pan and serve.

Spinach Cups   2 servings

4 oz. fresh spinach
¼ cup rice milk
2 large eggs, whisked
1 clove garlic, crushed
¼ tsp. sea salt
2 sprinkles pepper
1 tsp. olive oil for muffin cup greasing

1. Use 1 tsp. olive oil to grease 4 muffin cups.
2. Preheat oven to 400 degrees F.
3. Finely chop spinach.
4. In a large bowl mix all ingredients together well.
5. Divide mixture among 4 cups.
6. Bake 17-20 minutes, or until the spinach cups are set.
7. Cool in pan for 5 minutes, then loosen cups by running an oiled table knife down along the edges.

Spinach Scrambled Eggs   **2 servings**

1 tsp. olive oil
1 Tbsp. cilantro, sliced
1 Tbsp. scallions, chopped
1 handful fresh spinach, or 2 Tbsp. frozen chopped spinach
3 eggs
⅛ tsp. Italian herbs
¼ tsp. sea salt
2 dashes pepper

1. Place olive oil in iron skillet on medium heat for one minute.
2. Add cilantro, scallions, and spinach; sauté for 5 minutes.
3. Whisk eggs, herbs, pepper and salt.
4. Pour eggs into sautéed veggies.
5. Push eggs cooking with a spatula every 40-60 seconds.
6. When cooked to your liking, place on a plate, or on hash browns, or on gluten free toast.

Zucchini Scrambled Eggs 2 servings

1 tsp. olive oil
¼ cup sliced or shredded zucchini
¼ red bell pepper, cubed
½ scallion, sliced
3 eggs
¼ tsp. sea salt
2 dashes pepper
⅛ tsp. thyme
2 cherry tomatoes, sliced in four pieces each

1. Place olive oil in iron skillet on medium heat for one minute.
2. Sauté zucchini, red bell pepper, and scallion for five minutes.
3. Whisk eggs, salt, pepper, and thyme.
4. Add mixed eggs to skillet. As they cook, use a spatula to stir the eggs every 40-60 seconds.
5. Add sliced tomatoes and cook for one minutes
6. When cooked to your liking, remove from skillet and serve.

CHAPTER 5

Fruits and Vegetables Snacks and Meals

Braised Cabbage   **4 servings**   **VEGAN**

1 tsp. olive oil
1 cabbage, shredded (easiest when using a bag of shredded cabbage)
1 shallot, coarsely chopped
2 large carrots, shredded
¼ cup veggie stock (page12) or water
2 Tbsp. olive oil
¼ tsp. sea salt
2 dashes of pepper

1. Preheat oven to 350 degrees F.
2. Coat rectangular baking pan with oil (9"x13" is a good size).
3. Mix cabbage, shallots, and carrots in pan.
4. Mix stock, oil, salt, and pepper in a cup or small bowl.
5. Pour liquid mix over veggies, and mix again.
6. Bake at 350 for 25 minutes.
7. Finish with a broil for 2-3 minutes, lightly browning top of veggies.

Jicama Snack   　　　　　**4 servings**   　　　　**VEGAN**

1 medium Jicama
1 Tbsp. apple juice
¼ tsp. paprika
1 cucumber, sliced (optional addition)
1 cup blackberries (optional addition)

1. Peel and slice jicama into strips.
2. If desired, add sliced cucumber and blackberries.
3. Place in bowl, and sprinkle with paprika, pour on apple juice, mix and serve.

Spinach, Served Yummy   **4 servings**   **VEGAN**

1 tsp. olive oil
1 pound fresh spinach, cleaned and trimmed
2 tsp. apple juice
2 tsp. margarine
¼ tsp. nutmeg
2 grinds pepper

1. Rinse spinach
2. Cook spinach in large saucepan with olive oil over medium heat for 4 minutes, or until the leaves have wilted. Drain well.
3. Sprinkle with apple juice, margarine, nutmeg, and pepper. Serve.

Tomato or Bell Pepper Topped Zucchini   4 servings   VEGAN

1 Tbsp. olive oil
2 medium zucchini, sliced in half lengthwise
1 plum tomato, sliced or ¼ red bell pepper sliced
¼ tsp. sea salt
2 dashes pepper
1 tsp. dried basil

1. Preheat broiler.
2. Lightly brush oil on baking sheet and zucchini halves.
3. Broil 5 minutes.
4. Removed from oven and add remaining ingredients on top of zucchini slices.
5. Place back in oven and broil for 5 minutes.
6. Remove from oven and serve.

Trail Mix **8 servings** **VEGAN**

1 cup roasted salted sunflower seeds
1 cup roasted salted pumpkin seeds
½ cup dried cranberries
¼ cup shredded dry coconut
¼ cup dark chocolate chips

1. Mix all ingredients and store in a zip lock bag or glass container.

Twisted Cauliflower   **4 servings**   **VEGAN**

1 ½ cups veggie stock
2 bay leaves
2 cups cauliflower, cut into small chunks
1 tsp. mustard
½ tsp. dry dill

1. In a large iron skillet over medium heat, place veggie stock and Bay leaves for five minutes.
2. Stir cauliflower into iron skillet, cover, and simmer 6-8 minutes.
3. Add mustard and dill and mix.
4. Simmer for 2 more minutes.
5. Remove bay leaves.
6. Pull cauliflower from liquid and serve.

Veggie Burger   **4 servings**   **VEGAN**

1 shallot, diced
1 clove garlic, minced
1 ½ tsp. olive oil
1-15oz can black beans, rinsed
⅓ cup sunflower seeds
½ tsp. basil
1 tsp. sea salt
1 cup cooked brown Basmati rice

1. Place ½ tsp. olive oil in iron skillet on medium heat. Add shallots and garlic and sauté until translucent. Remove from skillet.
2. In large bowl with fork, mash black beans, sunflower seeds, basil, salt, and brown rice.
3. Add cooked shallot and garlic to bowl and mix well.
4. Form mixture into four patties.
5. Heat 1 tsp. olive oil in iron skillet on medium heat. Cook patties 4-6 minutes per side, until evenly browned on both sides.

Veggie Shake   **1 serving**   **VEGAN**

1 cup kale or spinach or baby romaine lettuce
½ cup of 2 fruits (i.e. frozen strawberries, blueberries, grapes, sliced apples, sliced apricots, mangos, etc.)
¼ apple juice
¼ cup water
1 tsp. honey or turbinado sugar
1 tsp. ground flax seed
¼ tsp. vanilla

1. Place all ingredients in a blender.
2. Blend on high until completely blended.
3. Pour in a cup and serve.

Veggie Stir Fry 4 servings VEGAN

1 Tbsp. olive oil
6 mushrooms, sliced
1 cup shredded carrots
2 scallions, sliced
1 clove garlic, crushed
1 celery stalk, diced
1 zucchini, shredded
1 Bock Choy, sliced
1 cup bean sprouts
1 Tbsp. cornstarch
¼ cup veggie stock
1 Tbsp. apple juice or cooking sherry
½ tsp. sea salt
¼ tsp. pepper
1 Tbsp. sesame oil

1. Place olive oil in iron skillet and heat on medium.
2. Place mushrooms in skillet and cook for 3 minutes.
3. Add carrots, green onions, garlic, and celery. Sauté for 5 minutes.
4. Add zucchini, bock Choy, and bean sprouts. Sauté for 5 minutes.
5. In a small bowl, mix cornstarch with 1 Tbsp. veggie stock. When mixed, add remaining veggie stock, cooking sherry, sea salt, pepper, and sesame oil and mix.
6. Pour liquid into iron skillet with veggies, turn heat up to high, and cook, stirring as liquid thickens.
7. When liquid is thickened and covers all veggies, remove from heat.
8. Delicious served over white rice, brown rice, or mixed rice.

CHAPTER 6

Rice and Potato Recipes

When simmering rice, cover pot with lid and do not stir. When rice is done, or other ingredients are added, the rice can then be stirred.

When recipes with butter or margarine are marked "vegan," choose vegan margarine to make it vegan. When recipes are marked vegan with butter or olive oil, choose olive oil to make it vegan.

Baked Potato Fries**2 servings****VEGAN**

3 medium potatoes
1 Tbsp. olive oil
Sea salt or garlic salt to taste

1. Preheat oven to 425 degrees F.
2. Hand rinse potatoes.
3. Slice to desired French fry size (French fry slicers make it easy).
4. Place in bowl of water, rinse thoroughly.
5. Drain water and add oil and salt to fries and stir to completely cover with olive oil.
6. Place on cookie sheet, spreading evenly with gaps between each fry to cook thoroughly.
7. Bake for 10 minutes, flip fries, bake for 10 more minutes.
8. Remove from oven and serve.

Basic Rice 　　　　　　　　**4 servings**　　　　**VEGAN**

1 tsp. olive oil or margarine
2 garlic cloves, crushed
½ tsp. sea salt
1 cup organic Basmati white rice
2 cups water or veggie stock (page 12)

1. Place olive oil or margarine, and crushed garlic and salt in saucepan over medium heat to lightly brown garlic.
2. Rinse rice thoroughly and drain.
3. Add rice to saucepan and stir for one minute.
4. Add water or veggie stock, raise temperature to high, and bring to boil.
5. Cover and reduce heat to low. Cook for 15 minutes.

Black Beans and Rice   4 servings   VEGAN

1 Tbsp. olive oil
1 shallot, diced
1 garlic clove, crushed
½ tsp. sea salt
¼ tsp. paprika or black pepper
1 cup white or brown Basmati rice
2 cups veggie stock
½ red or yellow bell pepper, diced
½ cup chopped tomatoes
1-15oz can black beans, rinsed
(½ pound sautéed ground beef - optional)

1. Place olive oil in cooking pot on medium heat.
2. Place shallot, garlic, salt and paprika in cooking pot and sauté for 4 minutes.
3. Raise heat to high and add rice and veggie stock. Bring to boil.
4. Reduce heat to low, cover and simmer 15 minutes for white rice, 35 minutes for brown rice.
5. Open lid and add peppers, tomatoes, and black beans.
6. Stir, place lid on pot, and simmer for 10 minutes.
7. Remove from heat, stir and serve.

Italian Rice **4 servings** **VEGAN**

2 cups veggie stock (page 12)
1 ½ tsp. Italian herbs
1 cup brown Basmati rice
2 cups kale or spinach (stems removed) and torn or chopped into small pieces

1. In a large cooking pot bring broth and seasoning to a boil.
2. Stir in rice and kale or spinach.
3. Cover and reduce heat to low.
4. Cook 30-40 minutes or until all liquid is absorbed.
5. Remove from heat, stir, and serve.

Hash Browns 2 servings **VEGAN**

2 potatoes
2 Tbsp. olive oil
½ tsp. sea salt

1. Shred potatoes or French fry slice then slice those into mini cubes.
2. Place olive oil in iron skillet over medium-high heat.
3. Blend salt and potatoes and add to skillet.
4. Sauté for 7-10 minutes.
5. Remove from pan and serve.

Herbed Garlic Potatoes   4 servings   VEGAN

6 medium new red potatoes, scrubbed
2 Tbsp. olive oil
2 cloves garlic, crushed
2 tsp. dried parsley
1 tsp. sea salt
¼ tsp. paprika or pepper

1. Preheat oven to 400 degrees F.
2. Cut each potato into cubes.
3. Combine oil and all other ingredients in a bowl and mix well.
4. Place potatoes in bowl and mix.
5. Place on cookie sheet, bake for 15 minutes.
6. Flip over potatoes and bake for an additional 10 minutes.
7. Remove from oven and serve.

Leeks Rice Casserole 2 servings VEGAN

1 cup veggie stock (page 12)
½ cup leeks, sliced
½ cup brown Basmati rice
1 clove garlic, crushed
1 shallot, diced
1 tsp. oregano
1 tsp. basil

1. Preheat oven to 300 degrees F
2. Mix all ingredients in a shallow baking dish.
3. Cover and bake for 45 minutes.
4. Remove cover and bake additional 15 minutes.
5. Remove from oven, stir, and serve.

Spanish Rice 4 servings VEGAN

2 Tbsp. canola oil
1 Tbsp. margarine
2 shallots, diced
2 garlic cloves, crushed
1 cup white Basmati rice
2 cups water
1 celery stalk, diced
1 medium tomato, diced
¼ tsp. oregano
1 tsp. sea salt

1. Heat oil and butter in cooking pot on medium-high heat for 1 minute.
2. Add Shallots, garlic, and celery and sauté for 4 minutes.
3. Add rice and sauté for one minute.
4. Add remaining ingredients and bring to a boil.
5. Reduce heat to low, cover and simmer for 18 minutes.
6. Remove from heat and let sit for 5 minutes.
7. Stir and serve.

Sweet Potato Circles 2 servings **VEGAN**

2 medium sweet potatoes or yams
2 tsp. olive oil
¼ tsp. sea salt

1. Preheat oven to 400 degrees F.
2. Peel, then slice sweet potatoes so they come out in circles ⅛ inch thick.
3. Place on a cookie sheet with olive oil and salt.
4. Bake 8 minutes, turn over and bake another 8 minutes.

Sweet Potato/Yam Fries   2 servings   VEGAN

2 medium sweet potatoes or yams
1 Tbsp. olive oil
½ tsp. sea salt

1. Preheat oven to 425 degrees F.
2. Peel sweet potatoes or yams and slice into strips (French fry size).
3. Place on cookie sheet with oil and salt and mix together.
4. Place in oven and bake for 10 minutes.
5. Remove from oven, flip over with spatula, and cook for 10 more minutes.
6. Remove from oven and serve.

Twice Baked Potatoes   **4 servings**   **VEGAN**

4 large potatoes
¼ cup rice milk
2 Tbsp. margarine
½ cup diced broccoli

1. Preheat oven to 425 degrees F.
2. Scrub, pierce, and bake potatoes for one hour.
3. Remove from oven and cut all potatoes in half.
4. Scoop out potato pulp into mixing bowl (leave potato half shells in place, set aside).
5. Mash potatoes in bowl.
6. Blend rice milk, margarine, and broccoli with mashed potatoes.
7. Place mashed potato mix back into the potato half shells.
8. Bake again at 425 for 15 minutes.

Yam Cubes **4 servings** **VEGAN**

3 yams, sliced into cubes
1 Tbsp. olive oil
¼ tsp. nutmeg
¼ tsp. sea salt

1. Preheat oven to 400 degrees.
2. Mix all ingredients in baking pan.
3. Bake for 25 minutes.
4. Remove from oven and serve.

CHAPTER 7

Poultry

Apple Chicken   **2 servings**

1 tsp. olive oil
2 chicken breasts, sliced in half
¼ tsp. sea salt
2 sprinkles pepper
1 apple, diced
1 shallot, diced
½ tsp. dried thyme
1 Tbsp. white vinegar or apple cider vinegar

1. Preheat oven to 375 degrees F.
2. Lightly oil shallow baking dish with olive oil.
3. Place chicken in dish and sprinkle with salt and pepper.
4. Arrange diced apple, diced shallot, and thyme over and around chicken.
5. Pour vinegar over all.
6. Place in oven and bake for 20 minutes, then check that chicken is fully cooked.
7. For extra flavor, broil 2-3 minutes.
8. Remove from oven and serve

Baked Chicken Breasts with Carrots   **2 servings**

2 chicken breasts
1 cup sliced carrots
1 Tbsp. olive oil
1 garlic clove, crushed
1 dash pepper
¼ tsp. sea salt
¼ tsp. paprika
¼ cup chicken stock (page 11)

1. Preheat oven to 400 degrees.
2. Place chicken breast in baking pan.
3. Place carrots around chicken.
4. Mix olive oil, garlic, pepper, sea salt, paprika, and chicken broth in a small bowl or cup. Pour over chicken and carrots.
5. Bake for 30-40 minutes. Remove from oven to check for chicken to be fully cooked, and serve.

Burrito Casserole   **4 servings**

1 tsp. olive oil
1 lb. chicken (or ground beef)
1 shallot, sliced
1 clove garlic, crushed
1 tsp. sea salt
⅛ tsp. pepper
¼ tsp. tarragon
¼ tsp. caraway seeds
1 small can sliced olives
1 8oz can tomato sauce
½ cup water
6 large gluten free tortillas or 1 cup tortilla chips

1. Preheat oven to 350 degrees F.
2. Place oil in iron skillet over medium heat.
3. Add meat, shallot, and garlic and cook until browned. (If using chicken, thinly slice after cooking).
4. Add salt, pepper, tarragon, caraway seeds, and olives. Sauté for 2 minutes.
5. In a 2 quart casserole, layer ½ of meat, ½ of tortillas, then last ½ of meat, and last ½ of tortillas.
6. Mix tomato sauce and water. Pour over casserole.
7. Cook in oven for 15 minutes.

Chicken Breast Sandwich   **2 servings**

2 tsp. olive oil
2 chicken breasts
Sea salt and pepper to taste
1 Tbsp. mayonnaise
4 slices cooked beef bacon (page 89)
Handful of lettuce
1 tomato, thinly sliced
Optional: thinly sliced avocado

1. Place olive oil in large iron skillet over medium heat.
2. Butterfly chicken breasts by cutting lengthwise through the middle of the breast *without cutting all the way through*, so it can be opened like a hinge.
3. Sprinkle butterflied chicken breasts with salt and pepper, and place opened up in iron skillet.
4. Cook 4-6 minutes on first side, until nicely browned, then flip chicken and cook on other side with lid on the pan, about 6 minutes.
5. When cooked, place on two plates. Spread thin layer of mayonnaise on the inside, layer bacon, lettuce, tomato and optional avocado.
6. Fold chicken breasts shut and serve. May be eaten warm or cold.

Chicken Fingers   **2 servings**

1 cup gluten free bread crumbs
1 tsp. garlic salt
¼ tsp. pepper
1 tsp. Italian herb mix
2 egg whites, beaten
2 chicken breasts, sliced into long pieces

1. Preheat oven to 400 degrees F.
2. Mix bread crumbs, garlic salt, pepper, and Italian herb mix in broad bowl or deep plate.
3. Grease a large cookie sheet with olive oil.
4. In batches of 4, dip chicken strips in egg whites, then bread crumb mix, and place on a greased cookie sheet.
5. Repeat until all chicken strips are placed on cookie sheet.
6. Bake for 7 minutes, flip over with spatula, and bake for 7 more minutes.
7. Delicious served with homemade honey mustard sauce (page 16) and home fries (page 55).

Chicken Shepherd's Pie **6 servings**

6 potatoes
4 tsp. olive oil
1 shallot, chopped
2 cloves garlic, crushed
2 chicken breasts, sliced into cubes
2 medium carrots, chopped
2 celery stalks, chopped
1 cup green beans cut into ½" pieces
1 cup chicken stock (page 11)
1 Tbsp. cornstarch
¼ cup rice milk
3 Tbsp. margarine
½ tsp. garlic salt

1. Preheat oven to 375 degrees.
2. Wash and slice potatoes into quarters and place in a large pot of water on high heat.
3. Bring potatoes in water to a boil; reduce heat to simmer for 15 minutes.
4. While Potatoes are cooking, place 1 Tbsp. of olive oil in iron skillet on medium head.
5. Add shallot and garlic to heated oil and sauté for 3 minutes.
6. Add sliced chicken breasts and sauté until cooked through.
7. Add carrots and celery, and sauté for five minutes.
8. Add green beans and sauté for two minutes.
9. Mix one Tbsp. of chicken stock with cornstarch until well blended, and then add remaining chicken stock as you mix them together.
10. Pour chicken stock into iron skillet and stir as the liquid thickens.
11. Drain cooked potatoes and place in a bowl with rice milk, margarine, and garlic salt.
12. Mash the potatoes, and then spread them across the top of thickened chicken mix.

13. Place in oven and bake for 25 minutes.
14. Complete by placing under broiler for 3 minutes.

Chicken Rice Stir Fry   **4 servings**

1 Tbsp. olive oil
1 scallion, sliced
2 chicken breasts, cubed
1 celery stalk, diced
¼ cup sliced mushrooms
½ cup shredded carrots
1 zucchini, diced
1 tsp. sesame oil
1 Tbsp. olive oil
1 cup cooked brown or white Basmati rice
2 Tbsp. soy sauce substitute (page 18)

1. Place olive oil in iron skillet over medium heat.
2. Add scallion and sauté for 2 minutes.
3. Add chicken breasts and sauté until fully cooked, approximately 10 minutes.
4. Add celery, mushrooms, and carrots and sauté for 5 minutes.
5. Add zucchini and sauté for 5 minutes.
6. Add remaining ingredients and sauté for 5 minutes.

Chicken-Spinach Stir Fry   **2 servings**

1 Tbsp. olive oil
1 shallot, sliced
2 chicken breasts cut into cubes
2 cups fresh spinach, washed and stems removed
2 oz. fresh mushrooms, washed and sliced
1 Tbsp. soy sauce substitute (page 18)
1 cup brown or white Basmati rice, cooked

1. Place olive oil in large iron skillet over medium heat.
2. Add shallot and sauté until translucent, about 5 minutes.
3. Add chicken and sauté until chicken is no longer pink and juices run clear, about 10 minutes.
4. Add spinach and mushrooms. Stir and continue cooking until vegetables reach desired doneness, about 5-7 minutes.
5. Add soy sauce substitute and sauté 2 minutes.
6. Serve over cooked rice.

Honey-Apple Juice Chicken Breasts   2 servings

2 Tbsp. honey
2 Tbsp. apple juice
3 Tbsp. substitute soy sauce (page 18)
3 cloves garlic, crushed
1 Tbsp. apple cider vinegar
2 chicken breasts

1. To make marinade, combine first five ingredients and mix well.
2. Cut chicken breasts in half and soak in marinade for 30-60 minutes.
3. Preheat oven to 400 degrees.
4. Place chicken on baking sheet and cook for 20 minutes.
5. Place marinade in small pot, bring to boil, and then reduce to simmer for 10 minutes to serve as a sauce on cooked chicken.
6. Broil chicken for 3 minutes to brown the tops.
7. Serve with boiled marinade.

Marinated Turkey Cutlets   **2 servings**

2 - 3, 4 oz. turkey cutlets
1 Tbsp. apple juice
2 tsp. olive oil
2 garlic cloves, crushed
¼ tsp. oregano
2 sprinkles of pepper
½ tsp. sea salt

1. Mix apple juice, olive oil, garlic, oregano, pepper, and sea salt in a marinating bowl or plate
2. Place turkey cutlets in marinade and let soak 30 minutes.
3. Turn oven on to Broil.
4. Place turkey cutlets on broiler pan and place in oven for 5 minutes.
5. Remove from oven and flip over all turkey cutlets.
6. Place back in oven and broil for 5-6 minutes, or until completely cooked inside.
7. Delicious served with Sweet Potato circles (page 63).

Mustard Molasses Chicken   **2 servings**

2 chicken breasts
1 shallot, thinly sliced
2 Tbsp. mustard
2 Tbsp. molasses

1. Preheat oven to 400 degrees.
2. Place chicken breasts in a baking pan.
3. Combine shallot, mustard and molasses and pour onto chicken breasts.
4. Place in oven and bake for 25 minutes, turning chicken over halfway through cooking time.
5. Yummy served with rice or baked potatoes.

Roasted Chicken 4-6 servings

1 whole chicken
1 cup carrots, sliced
4 medium potatoes, cubed
2 Tbsp. margarine, cubed
¼ tsp. marjoram
¼ tsp. rosemary
¼ tsp. sage
¼ tsp. oregano
2 scallions, sliced
½ tsp. sea salt
¼ tsp. pepper

1. Preheat oven to 400 degrees.
2. Rinse chicken (remove innards and save for making chicken stock).
3. Place chicken in large baking pan with carrots and potatoes.
4. Place margarine slices over chicken.
5. Sprinkle with remaining ingredients.
6. Bake for 1 hour. Remove from oven and test for complete cooking.
7. Let chicken cool for ten minutes, and slice for serving.

Roasted Chicken 2 with stuffing 4-6 servings

1 whole chicken
4 slices gluten free bread, toasted
2 ½ cups chicken stock (page 11)
1 tsp. marjoram
1 tsp. rosemary
1 tsp. sage
1 tsp. oregano
1 shallot, diced
2 shots of Worcestershire sauce
4 tsp. soy sauce substitute (page 18)
¼ cup melted margarine
4 potatoes, diced
2 Tbsp. margarine, diced
½ tsp. sea salt
¼ tsp. paprika
¼ tsp. pepper

1. Preheat oven to 400 degrees F.
2. Rinse chicken (remove innards and save for making chicken stock).
3. Dice toasted gluten free bread.
4. Mix 2 cups of chicken stock, marjoram, rosemary, sage, oregano, shallot, Worchester sauce, soy sauce substitute and melted margarine.
5. Add diced bread to create stuffing.
6. Place chicken on roasting pan and fill with stuffing.
7. Spread potatoes around chicken and pour on remaining ½ cup chicken stock.
8. Cover chicken with thick slices of margarine, sea salt, pepper, and paprika.
9. Place in oven and bake for 1 hour. Remove from oven and test for complete cooking. Larger chickens may need cooking up to 1 ½ hours.
10. Remove potatoes and stuffing. Slice chicken and serve.

Shallot Chicken   **2 servings**

1 Tbsp. olive oil
3 shallots, sliced
2 cloves garlic, crushed
2 chicken breasts, cubed
¾ tsp. sea salt
½ tsp. Italian seasoning

1. Place oil in iron skillet over medium heat.
2. Add shallots and garlic and sauté for 5 minutes.
3. Add cubed chicken breasts, sea salt, and Italian seasoning.
4. Sauté for approximately 15 minutes, until cooked and lightly browned, stirring every 2 minutes.
5. Tastes delicious served with white rice and vegetables.

Turkey Breasts with Stuffing   **4 servings**

2 slices gluten free bread, toasted
1 apple, diced
1 shallot, diced
1 celery stalk, diced
4 cloves garlic, crushed
½ tsp. sage
½ tsp. rosemary
¾ cup chicken stock (page 11)
2 turkey breasts
2 Tbsp. margarine

1. Preheat oven to 400 degrees.
2. Slice toasted gluten free bread into cubes.
3. In a large baking pan, blend bread cubes, apple, shallot, celery, garlic, sage, rosemary, and chicken stock. This is the stuffing.
4. Place turkey breasts on top of mixed stuffing.
5. Dice margarine, and spread across top of turkey breasts.
6. Place in oven and bake for 1 hour.
7. Remove turkey, slice for serving, and place back on top of stuffing.

Turkey Cutlet Casserole   **4 servings**

⅓ cup gluten free flour
½ tsp. sea salt
½ tsp. marjoram
⅛ tsp. pepper
1 ¼ pounds turkey cutlets
3 Tbsp. olive oil
1 red bell pepper, sliced
1 zucchini, halve lengthwise and sliced ¼ inch thick
8 oz. thinly sliced mushrooms
1 Tbsp. apple cider vinegar
½ cup apple juice
1 ¼ cup chicken stock (page 11)
1 cup cooked white Basmati rice

1. Mix gluten free flour, salt, marjoram and pepper.
2. Dredge cutlets in flour mixture.
3. Place 1 Tbsp. olive oil in large iron skillet on medium heat.
4. Add cutlets and sauté until golden brown and cooked through, 3-4 minutes per side.
5. Place cooked cutlets on a plate.
6. Place 1 Tbsp. olive oil in iron skillet and add red pepper and zucchini and sauté stirring occasionally until soft, about 5 minutes.
7. Add mushrooms and sauté until tender, about 3-4 minutes.
8. Pour in liquids and raise heat to high and boil for 2 minutes.
9. Lower heat to medium and return turkey to skillet, heating for 5 minutes.
10. Serve over rice.

Turkey Hash   **2 servings**

1 ½ cups turkey: cooked cubed turkey or cooked ground turkey
1 ½ tsp. olive oil
1 zucchini, diced
1 shallot, diced
1 sweet potato, diced and simmered in water for 5 minutes
½ tsp. thyme
½ tsp. sea salt
1 sprinkle of pepper
3 Tbsp. chicken stock (page 11)

1. Heat oil in iron skillet over medium heat.
2. Add shallot and sauté for 5 minutes.
3. Add turkey and sauté for 10 minutes, stirring every 2 minutes.
4. Add zucchini and sweet potato and cook for 10-12 minutes, stirring occasionally.
5. Add seasonings, stir.
6. Add chicken stock and simmer for 2-4 minutes.
7. Delicious served over rice.

Turkey Patties   **4 servings**

1 egg
¼ cup gluten free bread crumbs
1 scallion, diced
⅓ cup fresh parsley, sliced (or 1 tbsp. dry flakes)
⅛ tsp. marjoram
Sea salt and pepper to taste
1 lb. ground turkey
2 tsp. olive oil

1. In a bowl, mix egg, gluten free bread crumbs, scallion, parsley, marjoram, sea salt, and pepper.
2. Add ground turkey to bowl, mix, and shape into 4 large patties, or 8 small patties.
3. Place olive oil in large iron skillet over medium heat.
4. Place in iron skillet and cook 5-6 minutes on each side.
5. Remove from skillet and serve.
6. Yummy served with cooked yam fries and green beans.

Turkey Rolls   **2 servings**

4 turkey cutlets
4 slices homemade beef bacon (page 89)
6 Tbsp. gluten free bread crumbs
1 Tbsp. mayonnaise
1 Tbsp. olive oil
¼ cup apple juice
¼ cup chicken stock (page 11)

1. Top each cutlet with a slice of beef bacon and roll up jelly roll style, securing with two toothpicks per cutlet.
2. Brush turkey rolls with mayonnaise and dip in bread crumbs to coat fully.
3. Place olive oil in medium iron skillet over medium heat.
4. Add turkey rolls and sauté until browned all over, rotating ⅓ in the pan every two minutes to cook evenly, cooking for 6 minutes total.
5. Add juice, broth and butter or margarine and bring to a boil.
6. Cover, bring heat down to low, and simmer until turkey rolls are cooked through and sauce thickens, about 8 minutes.
7. Delicious served over cooked Rice pasta with broccoli on the side.

Turkey (or beef) Sausage 1   4 servings

1 lb. ground turkey or beef
1 ½ tsp. sea salt
¾ tsp. garlic powder
½ tsp. fennel seeds
½ tsp. pepper

1. Place oil in iron skillet over medium heat.
2. Blend spices and herbs.
3. Add meat and mix well (up to five minutes).
4. Shape into sausage patty shapes or meatballs.
5. Cook until fully cooked, 10-12 minutes.

Turkey Sausage 2   4 servings

2 tsp. olive oil
1 lb. ground turkey
½ cup gluten free bread crumbs
1 lightly beaten egg
1 tsp. sage
¾ tsp. sea salt
¼ tsp. paprika or pepper
⅛ tsp. nutmeg.

1. Place oil in iron skillet over medium heat.
2. Blend all ingredients.
3. Shape into sausage patty shapes or meatballs.
4. Sauté, turning over every 2 minutes or so, until completely cooked (10-12 minutes).

Turkey Stir Fry **2 servings**

2 tsp. cornstarch
2 tsp. canola oil
½ cup chicken stock (page 11)
2 tsp. olive oil
1 shallot, thinly sliced
¼ medium red bell pepper, thinly sliced
½ cup broccoli, in small pieces
2 Tbsp. sesame seeds
1 ½ cups turkey cutlets or breast, cooked and diced
½ tsp. sea salt

1. In a small bowl combine cornstarch, canola oil, and chicken broth.
2. Place olive oil in large iron skillet over medium heat.
3. Add shallot and sauté for 3 minutes.
4. Add bell pepper, broccoli, sesame seeds, and sea salt. Cook and stir until veggies reach desired crispness (7-9 minutes).
5. Stir in cooked turkey and mixed sauce and cook 4-6 minutes. Stir frequently as sauce thickens.
6. Remove from skillet to serve.
7. Delicious over cooked rice.

CHAPTER 8

Beef

Beef Bacon   **4 servings**

3 Tbsp. olive oil
2 Tbsp. apple cider vinegar
1 Tbsp. honey
2 garlic cloves, crushed
½ tsp. salt
¼ tsp. pepper
¼ tsp. Liquid Smoke or Worcestershire Sauce
1 lb. sliceable steak

1. Blend first 7 ingredients and place in a marinating container.
2. Slice beef as THINLY as possible. Best method is to have beef partially frozen, creating a stiffness of meat allowing for thin slicing.
3. Place beef in marinade for a minimum of one hour.
4. Beef bacon can be stored in the refrigerator for up to 4 days. It can be stored in the freezer for a month.
5. Cook beef bacon in an iron skillet coated with olive oil over medium heat.

Beef Ragu with Spaghetti Squash   **4 servings**

2 tomatoes
3 roasted red bell peppers
1 tsp. basil
1 Tbsp. olive oil
2 shallots, diced
3 cloves garlic, crushed
1 lb. ground beef or bison
½ tsp. sea salt
¼ tsp. pepper
1 spaghetti squash

1. In a mixer, blend tomatoes, roasted red peppers, and basil until saucy.
2. To cook spaghetti squash: cut in half, remove seeds, and microwave each half separately for 8 minutes; scrape spaghetti squash with a fork to create strands and place on a large plate or broad bowl.
3. To make Ragu, place olive oil in iron skillet on medium heat.
4. Add shallots and sauté for 2 minutes.
5. Add crushed garlic, beef, salt, and pepper and sauté for 5 minutes.
6. Add mixer blended sauce and turn heat to high while stirring beef and sauce.
7. Cook on high with frequent stirring for 10 minutes.
8. Serve Ragu over cooked spaghetti squash.

Beef Sliders   **4 servings**

1 Tbsp. olive oil
8 oz. mushrooms, washed and sliced
2 shallot, sliced into ring like shapes
¼ tsp. dried thyme
1 clove garlic, crushed
¼ tsp. sea salt
⅛ tsp. pepper
1 lb. ground beef
1 tomato, sliced
2 Tbsp. mayonnaise
8 gluten free slider rolls (gluten free bread can be sliced into correct shape and size)

1. Place olive oil in large iron skillet over medium heat.
2. Place mushrooms, shallots, and thyme in skillet and sauté for 10 minutes.
3. Add garlic, sea salt, and pepper and sauté for 2 minutes.
4. Place mushroom mix in a bowl or plate.
5. Form beef into 8 mini patties.
6. Cook beef patties in iron skillet on med high heat, approximately 4 minutes per side.
7. Top slider rolls with beef patties, mushroom mixture, and place slider rolls on top.
8. Delicious served with home fries and cooked veggies.

Broccoli Beef Stir Fry   **4 servings**

2 tsp. sesame oil
2 Tbsp. water
2 Tbsp. apple juice or cooking sherry
1 Tbsp. soy sauce substitute (page 18)
1 tsp. turbinado sugar
1 tsp. cornstarch
¾ lb. steak cut into ⅛" strips
1 Tbsp. olive oil
1 shallot, diced
1 clove garlic, crushed
1 lb. broccoli

1. In a small bowl, mix sesame oil, water, cooking sherry, soy sauce substitute and sugar. Set aside.
2. Place olive oil in large Iron skillet over medium heat.
3. Place shallot and garlic in iron skillet and sauté for 5 minutes.
4. Add sliced beef and sauté until cooked, 5 minutes.
5. Add broccoli and sauté for 5 minutes.
6. Add liquid mix and cook for 5 minutes, stirring frequently.
7. Yummy served with brown or white Basmati rice.

Marinated Steak   **4 servings**

3 Tbsp. olive oil
2 Tbsp. apple cider vinegar
1 Tbsp. honey
2 garlic cloves, crushed
½ tsp. sea salt
¼ tsp. pepper
1 ½ lbs. steak of your choice
1 tsp. olive oil

1. Mix olive oil, apple cider vinegar, honey, cloves, salt, and pepper in a marinating container.
2. Place steak, cut into four servings, in marinade and let marinate for 1 hour (it may rest in refrigerator up to 24 hours before cooking time).
3. Place olive oil in large iron skillet over medium heat.
4. Cook steak over medium heat for approximately 14 minutes - choose the amount of time that cooks the steak to your liking.
5. Serve.

Meatballs 1   **4 servings**

1 tsp. olive oil
1 lb. ground beef or bison
1 shallot, cubed
½ tsp. sea salt
¼ tsp. pepper
½ tsp. crushed rosemary
1 tsp. dried parsley or 1 Tbsp. fresh parsley
⅛ tsp. paprika

1. Place olive oil in medium iron skillet over medium heat.
2. Blend all remaining ingredients and shape into meatballs.
3. Place meatballs in iron skillet and sauté until fully cooked, approximately 15 minutes.
4. Delicious served with broccoli and home fries.

Meatballs 2   **4 servings**

1 Tbsp. olive oil
½ lb. ground beef
½ lb. ground turkey
1 clove garlic, crushed
¼ tsp. rosemary
¼ tsp. thyme
¼ tsp. oregano
¼ tsp. paprika
½ tsp. sea salt
1 diced shallot
½ cup gluten free bread crumbs
1 egg (optional)

1. Place olive oil in medium iron skillet over medium heat.
2. Blend all ingredients until thoroughly mixed.
3. Shape into meatballs.
4. Place meatballs in iron skillet and sauté until fully cooked, approximately 15 minutes.

Mini Meatloaf   **4 servings**

1 lb. ground beef
1 egg
¼ cup gluten free bread crumbs
1 celery stalk, very small diced
¼ cup finely grated carrots
½ tsp. sea salt
1 tsp. mustard
1 garlic clove, crushed
⅛ tsp. pepper

1. Preheat oven to 350 degrees.
2. Blend all ingredients until fully mixed.
3. Shape into 4 mini meatloafs.
4. Place in baking pan with ¼ cup of water.
5. Bake for 30 minutes.
6. Yummy served with baked potatoes and cooked veggies.

Protein Style Burger - No Bun   4 servings

1 tsp. olive oil
1 lb. ground beef
¼ tsp. sea salt
8 large lettuce leaves
1 large tomato, sliced
2 Tbsp. mayonnaise

1. Place olive oil in large iron skillet over medium heat.
2. Blend salt into ground beef and shape into four beef patties.
3. Place patties in skillet and cook for 5 minutes, flip over and cook 5 minutes.
4. On four plates place two large lettuce leaves each.
5. Place cooked beef patty on one half of lettuce leaves.
6. Spread with mayonnaise, top with tomato slices, and cover with other half of lettuce leaves.
7. Delicious served with home fries.

Sloppy Joes   **4 servings**

1 Tbsp. olive oil
1 red or yellow pepper, cubed
5 scallions, thinly sliced
1 cup carrots, shredded
1 ¼ lbs. ground beef (or turkey)
15 oz. canned tomato sauce
½ cup beef stock (page 10)
    or chicken stock (page 12) if using ground turkey
¼ cup dried cranberries
1 Tbsp. apple juice
½ tsp. sea salt
4 gluten free bagels, sliced and toasted

1. Place oil in large skillet over medium heat.
2. Add bell pepper and sauté 5 minutes
3. Add scallions and carrots, sauté 5 minutes
4. Add ground meat and sauté 8 minutes.
5. Stir in tomato sauce, beef stock, cranberries, apple juice, and salt.
6. Simmer until beef is cooked and sauce is thick and glossy, about 5 minutes.
7. Spoon beef mix onto toasted gluten free bagels and serve.

CHAPTER 9

Desserts and Snacks

Many of these muffins and bars can be stored in the freezer. I do this for a lunch snack. I pull it from the freezer in the morning and put it in my lunch bag for an afternoon snack.

In baking with eggs, if eggs are intolerable, you can replace each egg with 1 tablespoon of whole ground flaxseed + 3 tablespoons of water that have soaked for 30 minutes or more. You will see an example of this egg replacement in the zucchini rice flour muffins recipe.

Apple Crisp 6 servings VEGAN

4 small apples, sliced into thin slices
½ cup gluten free oatmeal
¼ cup turbinado sugar
¼ cup gluten free flour
¼ cup melted margarine

1. Preheat oven to 375 degrees.
2. Spread thinly sliced apples in pie plate.
3. In a bowl, mix oatmeal, sugar, gluten free flour, and melted margarine until well mixed.
4. Spread evenly across top of apples.
5. Cook for 40 minutes.
6. Remove from oven and cool for 5 minutes. Serve.

Apple Oat Flour Muffins   12 muffins

2 tsp. olive oil
1 egg
1 apple, shredded
⅓ cup rice milk
¼ cup melted margarine
½ cup turbinado sugar
1 tsp. nutmeg
1¼ cups sifted gluten free oat meal flour (can be made by shredding gluten free oats in blender)
½ cup rice flour
1 tsp. baking powder
1 tsp. baking soda

1. Preheat oven to 375 degrees.
2. Use 2 tsp. olive oil to grease muffin tins thoroughly (use an oil brush).
3. Blend egg, shredded apple, rice milk, and melted margarine.
4. Add sugar and nutmeg and blend thoroughly.
5. In separate bowl, mix oat flour, rice flour, baking powder, and baking soda.
6. Add dry ingredients to moist ingredients and mix well.
7. Fill each individual muffin tin, ⅔ full.
8. Bake in oven for 25 minutes. Test for complete cooking by poking a toothpick or skewer into a muffin, which should come out clean if cooking is complete.
9. Remove from oven and cool for five minutes.
10. Use a table knife to loosen and remove each muffin from muffin tin and place on cooling rack.

Banana Bread Muffins   **18 muffins**

2 tsp. olive oil
⅓ cup olive oil
⅔ cup turbinado sugar
2 eggs (or 2 Tbsp. crushed flaxseeds + 6 Tbsp. water soaked for 30 minutes)
¼ cup rice milk
1 tsp. vanilla
1½ cups gluten free flour
2 tsp. baking powder
1 tsp. nutmeg
½ tsp. sea salt
1 tsp. xanthan gum
1 ½ cups mashed bananas
½ cup dried cranberries

1. Preheat oven to 350 degrees.
2. Use 1 Tbsp. olive oil to grease muffin tins thoroughly. An oil brush works well to cover the inside of all muffin tins.
3. With a mixer, cream olive oil, turbinado sugar, eggs, rice milk and vanilla.
4. Add gluten free flour, baking powder, nutmeg, salt, and xanthan gum and mix by hand until well blended, but don't over mix.
5. Add mashed banana and dried fruit and mix in by hand.
6. Fill each individual muffin tin ⅔ full.
7. Bake for 20-25 minutes. Test for complete cooking by poking a toothpick or skewer into a muffin, which should come out clean if cooking is complete.
8. Use a table knife to loosen and remove each muffin from muffin tin and place on cooling rack.

Carrot Cake Muffins   **12 muffins**

1 Tbsp. olive oil
½ cup honey
½ cup turbinado sugar
½ cup melted margarine
¼ cup olive oil
2 eggs (or 2 Tbsp. crushed flaxseeds + 6 Tbsp. water soaked for 30 minutes)
1 ½ cups carrots, grated
½ cup apple sauce
1 cup gluten free flour
½ cup brown rice flour
2 Tbsp. ground flaxseed
1/2 tsp. xanthan gum
1/2 tsp. baking soda
½ tsp. baking powder

1. Preheat oven to 350 degrees.
2. Use 1 Tbsp. olive oil to grease muffin tins thoroughly. An oil brush works well to cover the inside of all muffin tins.
3. Blend honey, sugar, melted margarine, olive oil, and eggs.
4. Add carrots and applesauce and mix well; be sure honey is mixing in.
5. In separate bowl, mix flours, xanthan gum, baking soda, and baking powder.
6. Add dry ingredients to moist ingredients and mix well.
7. Fill each individual muffin tin ⅔ full.
8. Bake for 30 minutes. Test for complete cooking by poking a toothpick or skewer into a muffin, which should come out clean if cooking is complete.
9. Remove from oven and cool for five minutes.
10. Use a table knife to loosen and remove each muffin from muffin tin and place on cooling rack.

Chocolate Chip Cookies   **45 cookies**

2¼ cups gluten free flour
1 tsp. baking powder
1 tsp. baking soda
½ tsp. sea salt
¼ tsp. xanthan gum
¾ cup softened margarine
¾ cup turbinado sugar
½ cup white sugar
2 eggs (or 2 Tbsp. crushed flaxseeds + 6 Tbsp. water soaked for 30 minutes)
2 tsp. vanilla
2 cups dark chocolate chips

1. Preheat oven to 375 degrees.
2. Blend first 5 ingredients.
3. In separate bowl combine margarine, turbinado sugar, and white sugar and mix on medium speed of blender until creamy.
4. Add eggs and vanilla and mix for one minute.
5. Gradually add flour mixture on low speed until well mixed.
6. Stir in chocolate chips.
7. Place 2 inches apart on cookie sheet by rounded tablespoonful.
8. Bake for 9-12 minutes.
9. Remove from oven and cool for 2 minutes on cookie sheet before placing on cooling rack.

Granola Bars   28 mini granola bars   VEGAN

2 tsp. olive oil
½ cup + 2 TBSP margarine
½ cup honey
⅓ cup turbinado sugar
1 tsp. vanilla
1¼ cups gluten free flour
1 tsp. baking soda
4 cups gluten free oat meal
Optional: 1 cup add-ins such as dark chocolate chips, flax seeds, dried cranberries or blueberries, sunflower seeds, etc.)

1. Preheat oven to 350 degrees.
2. Use a kitchen brush to spread olive oil on a cookie sheet. Brush olive oil on wax paper the size of cookie sheet.
3. Soften margarine (microwave 10 seconds).
4. Blend butter, honey, sugar, and vanilla.
5. Add gluten free flour and baking soda and blend well.
6. Add oats and any other optional add-ins and blend, stirring thoroughly.
7. Pour granola mix on cookie sheet and spread out.
8. Place wax paper on top of granola mix and use a rolling pin to even out and flatten the granola mix on cookie sheet.
9. Remove wax paper.
10. Place granola mix on cookie sheet in oven and bake for 10 minutes.
11. Remove from oven and cool for one hour before cutting into granola mini bars, or larger granola bars.

Monster Cookies **3 dozen cookies**

½ cup margarine
1 ½ cups sunflower butter
1 cup turbinado sugar
1/2 cup honey or molasses
1 tsp. vanilla
3 eggs
2 tsp. baking soda
1 cup gluten free flour
½ cup dark chocolate chips
4 ½ cups gluten free oats

1. Preheat oven to 375 degrees.
2. Blend softened margarine, sunflower butter, sugar, molasses, vanilla, corn syrup and eggs.
3. Separately blend baking soda and gluten free flour, then add to butter/margarine mix and blend.
4. Blend in chocolate chips and gluten free oats.
5. Place by tablespoon on cooking sheet.
6. Place in oven and bake for 12 minutes.
7. Remove from oven, let sit on cookie sheet for 2 minutes, then move cookies onto cookie cooling racks.

Pumpkin Pie   **6-8 servings**

1 tsp. olive oil
4 gluten free slices of bread, toasted
1-15 oz. can organic pumpkin
1 cup canned coconut milk (it's almost as thick as cream)
1/2 cup rice milk
2 eggs
¾ cup turbinado sugar
1 tsp. nutmeg
¼ tsp. sea salt

1. Preheat oven to 375 degrees.
2. Spread olive oil in pie sheet.
3. Cube gluten free toast and spread around pie sheet.
4. Mix pumpkin, coconut milk, rice milk, eggs, turbinado sugar, nutmeg, and sea salt.
5. Pour pumpkin mix over gluten free bread in pie sheet.
6. Bake in the middle of the oven for 45-50 minutes, or until filling is set but center still trembles slightly.
7. Remove from oven and cool.
8. Slice into 6-8 pie slices and serve on mini plates (the bread cubes will not be settled down as a pie crust, but add a pie crust taste to the pie.)

Sesame Seed Sticks   **Fills One Cookie Sheet**

2 cups brown rice flour
1 cup sesame seeds
½ cup ground flax seeds
½ tsp. paprika
2 tsp. garlic powder
2 tsp. sea salt
10 crushed "sea salt and pepper crisps crackers" (optional)
4 Tbsp. sesame oil
4 Tbsp. olive oil
⅔ cup water

1. Preheat oven to 350 degrees.
2. Blend all dry ingredients.
3. In measuring cup, blend water, olive oil, and sesame oil.
4. Add wet ingredients to dry ingredient mix and blend until a dough forms.
5. Gather dough into a ball.
6. Place on the center of greased baking sheet.
7. Flatten (I use olive oil covered wax paper and a rolling pin) and score into sticks (I use an oiled knife).
8. Bake for 25 minutes, or until lightly brown and crispy.
9. Cool for one hour and break along score lines.
10. Store in glass container for up to one week.

Sunflower Coconut Cookie Rounds　　　　**2 dozen**

1 cup sunflower butter
½ cup coconut flour
⅔ cup unsweetened shredded coconut
4 Tbsp. coconut milk
4 Tbsp. coconut oil
1 Tbsp. turbinado sugar

1. Blend sunflower butter, coconut flour, ⅓ cup shredded coconut, coconut milk, coconut oil and turbinado sugar with a mixer until well blended.
2. Mold into bite size balls
3. Roll balls in ⅓ cup shredded coconut.
4. Refrigerate 30 minutes.
5. Enjoy!

Yam Muffins   **18 muffins**

1 Tbsp. olive oil
1 large cooked yam, mashed
⅔ cup rice milk
¼ cup canola oil
2 large beaten eggs (or 2 Tbsp. crushed flaxseeds + 6 Tbsp. water soaked for 30 minutes)
1 tsp. vanilla
½ cup turbinado sugar
½ tsp. nutmeg
2 cups rice flour
1 tsp. baking powder
1 tsp. baking soda
½ tsp. xanthan gum
½ cup dried cranberries

1. Preheat oven to 425 degrees.
2. Use 1 Tbsp. olive oil to grease muffin tins thoroughly. An oil brush works well to cover the inside of all muffin tins.
3. Blend yam, rice milk, canola oil, eggs, and vanilla.
4. Add turbinado sugar and nutmeg.
5. In separate bowl mix flour, baking powder, baking soda and xanthan gum.
6. Add dry ingredients to moist ingredients and mix well.
7. Add dried cranberries and mix well.
8. Fill each individual muffin tin ⅔ full.
9. Bake for 20-25 minutes. Test for complete cooking by poking a toothpick or skewer into a muffin, which should come out clean if cooking is complete.
10. Remove from oven and cool for five minutes.
11. Use a table knife to loosen and remove each muffin from muffin tin and place on cooling rack.

Waffles **10 waffles**

1¾ cups gluten free flour
2 tsp. baking powder
1 tsp. sea salt
3 eggs, separated
¾ cup rice milk or coconut milk
1 tsp. vanilla
4 Tbsp. melted butter or margarine

1. Preheat waffle iron and coat top and bottom with oil.
2. Blend gluten free flour, baking powder, and sea salt.
3. Add 3 egg yolks, rice milk or coconut milk, vanilla, and melted butter or margarine and blend until well mixed.
4. In separate bowl, whip egg whites until fluffy.
5. Fold fluffy egg whites into waffle mix until gently blended.
6. Fill waffle iron with waffle mix and cook for 3-4 minutes.
7. Delicious served with ½ cup frozen blueberries cooked in small saucepan for 10 minutes with ¼ cup of water, 1 Tbsp. turbinado sugar, and 1 Tbsp. cornstarch mixed with one cup of water.

Zucchini Rice Flour Muffins   2 dozen   VEGAN

1 Tbsp. olive oil
2 medium zucchini, shredded
2 tsp. vanilla
½ cup honey
½ cup turbinado sugar
2 Tbsp. whole ground flaxseed + 6 Tbsp. water soaked for 30 minutes
¼ cup olive oil
¼ cup margarine, melted
½ cup rice milk
⅓ cup cocoa powder (optional)
½ tsp. nutmeg (optional)
1 tsp. xanthan gum
1 tsp. baking soda
2 ½ cups rice flour

1. Preheat oven to 350 degrees.
2. Use 1 Tbsp. olive oil to grease muffin tins thoroughly. An oil brush works well to cover the inside of all muffin tins.
3. Mix shredded zucchini, vanilla, honey, turbinado sugar, flaxseed + water, olive oil, and rice milk until well blended.
4. In separate bowl, mix xanthan gum, baking soda, and rice flour.
5. Add dry ingredients to wet ingredients and blend by hand until well mixed.
6. Fill each individual muffin tin ⅔ full.
7. Bake for 40 minutes. Test for complete cooking by poking a toothpick or skewer into a muffin, which should come out clean if cooking is complete.
8. Remove from oven and cool for 5 minutes.
9. Use a table knife to loosen and remove each muffin from muffin tin and place on cooling rack.

Chocolate Frosting for 2 dozen Muffins

2 cups powdered sugar
¼ cup coconut oil, melted
¼ cup margarine, softened
1 tsp. vanilla
¼ cup cocoa powder
3-6 Tbsp. rice milk

1. Place first five ingredients plus 3 tablespoons rice milk in mixing bowl.
2. Blend with blender.
3. Add rice milk as needed for best consistency of frosting.
4. Cover zucchini muffins with frosting when cooled after cooking.

Appendix A

This is a list of foods that are not in this cookbook.
These are foods that I *cannot* eat due to migraines, lactose intolerance, and sensitive stomach:

- Caffeine
- Chocolate – I do include milk free, soy free dark chocolate chips in only 4 recipes, & cocoa powder in two recipes, a once in a while treat to share with others
- Monosodium Glutamate
- Processed meats and fish
- Cheese and other dairy products
- Nuts (some recipes I list nuts as an option to seeds if you can tolerate them)
- Alcohol - I do include cooking sherry in 3 recipes, you can replace with apple juice
- Certain fruits - citrus, tangerines, pineapples, raisins, dried fruit with sulfites, red plums, papayas, passion fruit, figs, and dates
- Avocados are in one recipe as an option for people who can tolerate them, but they are on the migraine list.
- Certain vegetables - onions, pea pods, sauerkraut, broad Italian beans, fava beans, navy beans, and lentils (replace these with black beans, leeks, scallions, shallots, and garlic)
- Fresh-Yeast raised baked goods and wheat
- Aspartame and NutraSweet (aren't they bad for everyone?)
- Soy products (but soy oil is ok)

I also don't use milk or cheese in my recipes, due to lactose intolerance. Many recipes list margarine, but you can use butter if you tolerate it. I use small amounts of butter occasionally, but soy free margarine or Earth Balance soy free buttery sticks are a good option for butter. With these recipes, I have an incredible reduction in migraines and upset stomach!

Appendix B

This is the list of foods I have come up with that I *can* eat, and that you will find in this cookbook. You can utilize the elimination diet to know what you can and can't eat. Some foods that I can eat I eat only once a week to prevent migraines: catsup, dark chocolate chips, coco powder, bananas, tomatoes, anything related to coconut, and mushrooms. The following foods should all be found in this cookbook. I thoroughly read ingredients listed in any processed foods, such as gluten free bread, gluten free flour, catsup, mayonnaise, and mustard to find the brand that works for me.

Apples	Apple Juice	Apple Sauce
Apricots	Baking Powder	Baking Soda
Bagels, Gluten Free	Bananas	
Basmati Brown Rice	Basmati White Rice	Barley
Basil	Bay Leaves	Bean Sprouts
Beef	Beets	
Bell Peppers (Yellow, Red, or Orange)		Bison
Black Beans	Blackberries	Bok Choy
Bread, Gluten Free	Broccoli	
Brown Rice Flour	Cabbage	Canola Oil
Caraway Seeds	Carrots	Catsup
Cauliflower	Celery	Chicken
Cilantro	Cocoa Powder	
Coconut Flour	Coconut Milk	Coconut
Coriander	Cornstarch	
Cranberries, dried	Cranberry Juice	Cucumbers
Dark Chocolate Chips (lactose free, soy free)		Dill
Eggs	Fennel Seeds	Flax Seeds
Garlic	Gluten Free Flour	Grapes
Grape Juice	Green Beans	Honey
Italian Herbs	Jicama	Kale
Leeks	Lettuce (many varieties)	
Liquid Smoke	Mangos	
Margarine (I use Earth Balance Soy Free Buttery Sticks)		

Marjoram	Mayonnaise	Melons
Molasses	Mung Bean Sprouts	
Mushrooms	Mustard	Nectarines
Nutmeg	Oatmeal, Gluten Free	
Oat-flour, Gluten Free	Olives	Olive Oil
Oregano	Paprika	Parsley
Peaches	Pepper	Potatoes
Powdered Sugar	Pumpkins	Pumpkin Seeds
Quiche	Radish	Rice Crackers
Rice Flour	Rice Flour	Rice Milk
Rice Noodles	Rice Pasta	Rosemary
Sage	Scallions	Sea Salt
Sesame Seeds	Shallots	Spaghetti Squash
Spinach	Soy Sauce Substitute	
Sunflower Butter	Sunflower oil	Sunflower Seeds
Sweet Potatoes	Tarragon Leaves	Thyme
Tomatoes	Tortillas, Gluten Free	
Tortilla Chips, Gluten Free		Tuna Fish
Turbinado Sugar	Turkey	Vanilla
Vinegar	White Tea	White Vinegar
White Sugar	Worcestershire Sauce	
Xanthan Gum	Yams	Zucchini

Appendix C

5 Week Dinner List

Week 1
Sun: Chinese Chicken Salad and Basic Rice
Mon: Mini Meatloaf, Baked Potatoes, Broccoli
Tues: Turkey Patties, Yam Fries, Mediterranean Salad
Wed: Shallot Chicken, Basic Rice, Braised Cabbage
Thurs: Marinated Steak, Herbed Garlic Potatoes, Mixed Veggies
Fri: Chicken Fingers, Twice Baked Potatoes, Green Beans
Sat: Turkey Hash, Italian Rice

Week 2
Sun: Chicken Shepherd's Pie
Mon: Meatballs, Hash Browns, Broccoli
Tues: Turkey Stir Fry, Italian Rice
Wed: Chicken Breast Sandwich, Yam Cubes
Thurs: Beef Sliders, Baked Potato Fries, Mixed Veggies
Fri: Apple Chicken, Basic Rice, Spinach Served Yummy
Sat: Turkey Sausage 1 or 2, Yam fries, Green Beans

Week 3
Sun: Chicken Spinach Stir Fry
Mon: Chili Con Carne, Corn, Basic Rice
Tues: Turkey Cutlet Casserole
Wed: Mustard Molasses Chicken, Cooked Carrots, Baked Potatoes
Thurs: Protein Style Hamburgers, Baked Home Fries, Broccoli
Fri: Waldorf Chicken Salad, Toasted Gluten Free Bread
Sat: Veggie Stir Fry, Basic Rice or Black Beans & Rice

Week 4
Sun: Roasted Chicken 1 or 2, optional: Baked Potatoes, Mixed Veggies
Mon: Sloppy Joes, Toasted Gluten Free Bread, Green Beans
Tues: Turkey Rolls, Rice Pasta, Braised Cabbage
Wed: Baked Chicken Breasts with Carrots, Herbed Garlic Potatoes
Thurs: Beef Barley Stew OR Old Fashion Beef Stew
Fri: Veggie Burger, Twisted Cauliflower
Sat: Hearty Sausage Bean Soup

Week 5
Sun: Chicken Soup
Mon: Beef Ragu with Spaghetti Squash
Tues: Marinated Turkey Cutlets, Sweet Potato Circles, Twisted Cauliflower
Wed: Mustard and Molasses Chicken, Baked Potato Fries, Tomato or Bell Pepper Topped Zucchini
Thurs: Broccoli Beef Stir Fry, Basic Rice
Fri: Burrito Casserole, Jicama Snack
Sat: Turkey Breast w/ Stuffing, Baked Yams, Spinach Served Yummy

There are many more recipes in this cookbook, not listed on this five week dinner plan. This plan is simply an example of how to vary the food you eat over five weeks when on a limited diet. Some foods listed are not from a recipe: baked potatoes, rice pasta, and basic vegetables such as broccoli, cooked carrots, corn, green beans, and mixed veggies. These are simply foods you cooked for dinner. There are so many choices in this 5 week plan that it doesn't feel like a limited diet; it feels like a nutritious-delicious diet!

INDEX

A
Almond Milk, 5
Apple, 27, 28, 35, 53, 67, 82, 99, 100
Apple Chicken Recipe, 67
Apple Cider Dressing, 28
Apple Cider Dressing Recipe, 14
Apple Cider Vinegar, 5, 14, 17, 18, 31, 34, 67, 76, 83, 89, 93
Apple Crisp Recipe, 99
Apple Juice, 5, 14, 17, 18, 31, 34, 54, 67, 76, 83, 89, 92, 93
Apple Juice Dressing Recipe, 15
Apple Oat Flower Muffins Recipe, 100
Apple Sauce, 102
Apricots, 8, 53
Avocado, 70

B
Bagels, gluten free, 98
Baked Chicken Breasts with Carrots Recipe, 68
Baked Potato Fries Recipe, 55
Baking Powder, 100-103, 109, 110
Baking Soda, 100, 102-105, 109, 111
Banana, 101
Banana Bread Muffins Recipe, 101
Barley, 19
Basic Rice Recipe, 56
Basil, 14, 25, 26, 33, 40, 49, 52, 61, 90
Basmati Rice, 22, 52, 56-58, 61, 62, 74, 75, 83
Bay Leaves, 10, 12, 19, 23, 24, 51
Bean Salad Recipe, 32
Bean Sprouts, 54
Beef, 19, 20, 57, 69, 91, 94, 95, 96, 97, 98

Beef Bacon, 40, 70, 86
Beef Bacon Recipe, 89
Beef Barley Stew Recipe, 19
Beef Bones, 10
Beef Fat, 10
Beef Ragu with Spaghetti Squash Recipe, 90
Beef Stew, Old Fashioned Recipe, 20
Beef Stock, 13, 19, 20, 98
Beef Stock Recipe, 10
Beef Sliders Recipe, 91
Beets, 28, 32
Bell Peppers, 8, 24, 32, 34, 38, 41, 45, 49, 57, 83, 88, 90, 98
Bell Pepper Topped Zucchini Recipe, 49
Bison, 90, 94
Black Beans, 23, 24, 26, 32, 52, 57
Black Bean Salad Recipe, 26
Black Beans & Rice Recipe, 57
Black Berries, 47
Blue Berries, 53, 104
Bok Choy, 38, 41, 54
Bok Choy Black Beans Recipe, 57
Bok Choy & Scrambled Eggs Recipe, 38
Braised Cabbage Recipe, 46
Bread, 5
Bread Crumbs, gluten free, 7, 71, 86, 95
Bread, gluten free, 82, 85, 87, 91, 96, 106
Broccoli, 5, 41, 65, 88, 92
Broccoli Beef Stir Fry Recipe, 92
Broccoli Florets, 36
Broccoli Quiche Recipe, 36
Broccoli Slaw Salad Recipe, 27
Broccoli Stalk, 27, 28
Brown Basmati Rice, 22, 52, 57, 58, 61, 74, 75
Brown Rice Flour, 5
Burrito Casserole Recipe, 69

Butter, 5

C
Cabbage, 46
Caraway Seed, 23, 69
Carrots, 8, 11, 12, 19, 20, 22, 27, 28, 37, 41, 46, 54, 68, 72, 74, 79, 96, 98, 102
Carrot Cake Muffins Recipe, 102
Carrot Scrambled Eggs Recipe, 37
Cauliflower, 5, 41, 51
Celery, 7, 10, 11, 12, 22, 30, 34, 35, 37, 54, 62, 74, 82, 96
Chicken Bones, 11
Chicken Breasts, 22, 28, 29, 35, 67-72, 74-76, 78, 81
Chicken Breasts Baked with carrots Recipe, 68
Chicken Breasts Sandwich Recipe, 70
Chicken Breast with Honey & Apple Juice Recipe, 76
Chicken Fingers Recipe, 71
Chicken Rice Stir Fry Recipe, 74
Chicken, Roasted Recipes, 79, 80
Chicken Salad Recipes, 28, 29, 35
Chicken, Shepard's Pie Recipe, 72
Chicken Soup Recipe, 22
Chicken Spinach Stir Fry Recipe, 75
Chicken Stock Recipe, 11
Chicken Stock, 22, 25, 68, 72, 80, 82-84, 86, 88, 98
Chicken with Mustard & Molasses Recipe, 78
Chicken with Shallots Recipe, 81
Chicken, Whole Chicken Recipes, 79, 80
Chili Con Carne Recipe, 23
Chinese Chicken Salad Recipe, 29
Chocolate Chips, 50, 103, 104, 105
Chocolate Chip Cookies Recipe, 103
Chocolate Frosting Recipe, 112
Cilantro, 44
Cocoa Powder, 111, 112

Coconut Cookie Rounds Recipe, 108
Coconut Flour, 108, 111, 112
Coconut Milk, 5, 106, 108, 110
Coconut, shredded, 108
Cookies, 103, 104, 105, 108
Cooking Sherry, 20, 54, 92
Cornstarch, 54, 72, 92
Crackers, Sea Salt & Pepper, 107
Cranberries, dried, 27, 28, 30, 50, 98, 101, 104, 109
Cranberry Juice, 6
Cranberry Tuna Salad Recipe, 30
Cucumber, 31, 33, 47

D
Dijon Mustard, 16
Dill, 51
Dressing for Salads, 14-17, 29, 31

E
Eggs, 6, 36-45, 85, 87, 95, 96, 100-103, 105, 106, 109, 110
Egg Recipes, 36-45
Egg Whites, 71

F
Fennel Seeds, 87
Flax Seeds, 6, 101-104, 107, 109, 111
Flaxseed Replacing Eggs, 6, 99, 101-103, 109, 111
Fries, Potatoes Recipe, 55
Fries, Yam Recipe, 64
Fruit, 8, 27, 28, 30, 35, 47, 50, 53, 67, 82, 98-102, 104, 109
Fruit Preparation, 8

G
Garlic, 12, 15, 17, 19, 20, 22, 24, 25, 29, 43, 52, 54, 56, 57, 60-62, 68, 69, 72, 76, 77, 81, 82, 87, 89, 90-93, 95, 96

Garlic Powder, 24, 107
Garlic Salt, 55, 71, 72
Gluten Free Bagels, 98
Gluten Free Bread, 5, 7, 80, 82, 91, 106
Gluten Free Bread Crumbs, 86, 87, 95
Gluten Free Flour, 5, 13, 19, 20, 83, 99-105, 110
Gluten Free Oatmeal, 99, 104, 105
Gluten Free Oatmeal Flour, 8
Gluten Free Tortillas, 69
Gluten Free Tortilla Chips, 69
Granola Bars Recipe, 104
Grapes, 8, 35, 53
Grape Juice, 5, 6
Gravy, Homemade Recipe, 13
Green Beans, 19, 22, 32, 41, 72
Ground Beef, 23, 90, 91, 94, 95, 96, 97, 98
Ground Flaxseeds, 53, 102, 107, 111
Ground Turkey, 85, 87, 84, 87, 95

H
Hash Browns, 39
Hash Browns Recipe, 59
Hearty Sausage & Bean Soup Recipe, 24
Herbs, 5
Herbed Garlic Potatoes Recipe, 60
Homemade Gravy Recipe, 13
Honey, 16, 53, 76, 81, 93, 102, 104, 105, 111
Honey-Apple Juice Chicken Breasts Recipe, 76
Honey Mustard Dressing, 26, 27
Honey Mustard Dressing Recipe, 16

I
Italian Herbs, 41, 44, 58, 71, 81
Italian Rice Recipe, 58

J
Jicama Snack Recipe, 47

K
Kale, 5, 38, 41, 53, 58
Kale Scrambled Eggs Recipe, 38

L
Leeks, 9, 12, 39, 61
Leeks Rice Casserole Recipe, 61
Leeks Scrambled Eggs Recipe, 39
Lemon Juice, 6
Lettuce, 28, 29, 31, 34, 36, 53, 70, 97
Lettuce, Romaine, 31
Liquid Smoke, 89

M
Mango, 53
Margarine, 5, 13, 19, 36, 48, 56, 62, 65, 72, 79, 80, 82, 99, 100, 102-105, 110-112
Marinated Steak Recipe, 93
Marinated Turkey Cutlets Recipe, 77
Marjoram, 23, 79, 80, 83, 85
Mayonnaise, 30, 34, 35, 70, 86, 91, 97
Meatballs Recipes, 94, 95
Mediterranean Salad and Dressing Recipe, 31
Milk, 5
Mini Meat Loaf Recipe, 96
Mixed Bean Salad Recipe, 32
Molasses 18, 78, 105
Monster Cookies Recipe, 105
Muffins, 100-102, 109, 111
Mushrooms, 20, 22, 40, 41, 54, 74, 75, 83, 91
Mustard, 51, 78, 96

Mustard Molasses Chicken Recipe, 79

N
Non-Soy Sauce Recipe, 18
Non-Soy Sauce Substitute, 5
Nutmeg, 36, 48, 66, 87, 100, 101, 106, 109, 111
Nuts, 5

O
Oatmeal Flour, Gluten Free, 8, 100
Oatmeal, Gluten Free, 99, 104, 105
Old Fashioned Beef Stew Recipe, 20
Olives, 26, 69
Olive Oil, 14-17, 19, 20, 22-24, 28, 29, 31, 33-46, 48, 49, 52, 54-56, 57, 59, 60, 63, 64, 66-70, 72, 74, 75, 77, 81, 83-95, 97, 98, 100-102, 104, 106, 107, 109, 111
Onions, 5
Orange Juice, 6
Oregano, 19, 22, 38, 40, 61, 62, 77, 79, 80, 95
Organic Pumpkin, 106
Organic Salad Greens, 26, 28, 29, 35

P
Paprika, 10, 47, 57, 60, 68, 80, 87, 94, 95, 107
Parsley, 7, 10, 11, 12, 20, 25, 31, 60, 85, 94
Peanut Butter, 5
Pepper, 11, 13, 18, 20, 24, 29, 31, 33, 36-38, 41-47, 49, 54, 57, 60, 67-69, 71, 77, 79, 83, 84, 85, 87, 89, 90, 91, 93, 94, 96
Pizza Frittata Recipe, 40
Potatoes, 20, 55, 59, 60, 65, 72, 79, 80
Potato Fries Recipe, 55
Potato Starch, 5
Powdered Sugar, 112
Pumpkin, 106
Pumpkin Pie Recipe, 106

Pumpkin Seeds, 5, 50
Protein Style Burger Recipe, 97

Q
Quiche Recipe, 41

R
Radish, 31
Red Potatoes, 60
Rice, 22, 52, 56-58, 61, 62, 74, 75, 83
Rice & Black Beans Recipe, 57
Rice Crackers, 29, 41
Rice Flour, 5, 100, 109, 111, 102, 107
Rice Milk, 5, 36, 43, 65, 72, 100, 101, 106, 109, 110-112
Rice Noodles, 29
Rice Recipe, Basic, 56
Roasted Chicken Recipes, 79, 80
Romaine Lettuce, 31, 53
Rosemary, 79, 80, 82, 94, 95

S
Sage 79, 80, 82, 87
Salads, 26-35
Salad Dressing Recipes, 14-17, 29, 31
Sandwich, Chicken Breast Recipe, 70
Scallions, 5, 9, 14, 23, 29, 31, 34, 37, 41, 42, 44, 45, 54, 74, 79, 85, 98
Sea Salt, 5, 10-14, 17-20, 22-24, 28, 29, 31, 33-38, 42-46, 49, 52, 54-57, 59, 60, 62-64, 66-69, 77, 79-81, 83-85, 87-91, 93-98, 101, 103, 106 107, 110
Seeds, 5, 50
Sesame Oil, 17, 18, 29, 54, 74, 92, 107
Sesame Salad Dressing Recipe, 17
Sesame Seeds, 17, 29, 88, 107
Sesame Seeds Sticks Recipe, 107

Shallots, 5, 10-12, 19, 20, 22, 24, 30, 33, 38, 46, 52, 57, 61, 62, 67, 69, 72, 75, 78, 80-82, 84, 88, 90, 91, 92, 94, 95
Shallot Chicken Recipe, 81
Sloppy Joes Recipe, 98
Spaghetti Squash, 9, 25, 42, 90
Spaghetti Squash Omelet Recipe, 42
Spanish Rice Recipe, 62
Spices, 5
Spinach, 5, 41, 43, 44, 48, 53, 58, 75
Spinach Cups Recipe, 43
Spinach Scrambled Eggs Recipe, 44
Spinach Served Yummy Recipe, 48
Soup, Chicken Recipe, 22
Soup, Hearty Sausage & Beans Recipe, 24
Soup, Turkey Sausage Recipe, 25
Soy Sauce, 5
Soy Sauce Substitute, 17, 18, 20, 74-76, 80, 92
Soy Sauce Substitute Recipe, 18
Stacker Salad Recipe, 33
Steak, 89, 92, 93
Stew, Beef Barley Recipe, 19
Stew, Old Fashioned Beef Recipe, 20
Strawberries, 8, 53
Sunflower Butter, 5, 105, 108
Sunflower Seeds, 5, 27-29, 35, 50, 52, 104
Sunflower Coconut Cookie Rounds Recipe, 108
Sweet Potatoes, 63, 64, 84
Sweet Potato Circles Recipe, 63
Sweet Potato Fries Recipe, 64

T
Tarragon, 69
Thyme, 12, 20, 22, 24, 45, 67, 84, 91, 95
Tomatoes, 12, 23-26, 31, 33, 40, 45, 49, 57, 62, 70, 90, 91, 97
Tomato Paste, 20, 23

Tomato Sauce, 69, 98
Tomato or Bell Pepper Topped Zucchini Recipe, 49
Tortilla Chips, gluten free, 69
Tortillas, gluten free, 69
Trail Mix Recipe, 50
Tuna Fish, 30
Tuna Salad Recipe, 30
Turbinado Sugar, 14, 29, 34, 53, 92, 99-106, 108, 109, 111
Turkey Breasts, 82, 88
Turkey Breasts w/Stuffing Recipe, 82
Turkey Cutlets, 34, 77, 83, 84, 86, 88
Turkey Cutlet Casserole Recipe, 83
Turkey, Ground, 84, 85, 87, 95
Turkey Hash Recipe, 84
Turkey Patties Recipe, 85
Turkey Rolls Recipe, 86
Turkey Salad Recipe, 34
Turkey Sausage Recipes, 87
Turkey Sausage, 24, 25, 40, 87
Turkey Sausage Soup Recipes, 24, 25
Turkey Stir Fry Recipe, 88
Twice Baked Potatoes Recipe, 65
Twisted Cauliflower Recipe, 51

V
Vanilla, 53, 101, 103-105, 109-112
Veggie Burger Recipe, 52
Veggie Shake Recipe, 53
Veggie Stir Fry Recipe, 54
Veggie Stock Recipe, 12
Veggie Stock, 24, 46, 51, 54, 56-58, 614
Vinegar, 5

W
Waffles Recipe, 110

Waldorf Chicken Salad Recipe, 35
Wheat, 5
White Vinegar, 5, 14, 16-18, 29, 67
White Basmati Rice, 56, 57, 62, 74, 75, 83
White Sugar, 103
Wine, 5
Worcestershire Sauce, 80, 89

X
Xanthan Gum, 101-103, 109, 111

Y
Yams, 63, 64, 66, 109
Yam Cubes Recipe, 66
Yam Fries Recipe, 64
Yam Muffins Recipe, 109

Z
Zucchini, 8, 41, 45, 49, 54, 74, 83, 84, 111
Zucchini Rice Flour Muffins Recipe, 111
Zucchini Scramble Eggs Recipe, 45

Made in the USA
San Bernardino, CA
12 February 2016